DC SUPER-VILLAINS

THE OFFICIAL COLORING BOOK

INSIGHT
EDITIONS

SAN RAFAEL • LOS ANGELES • LONDON

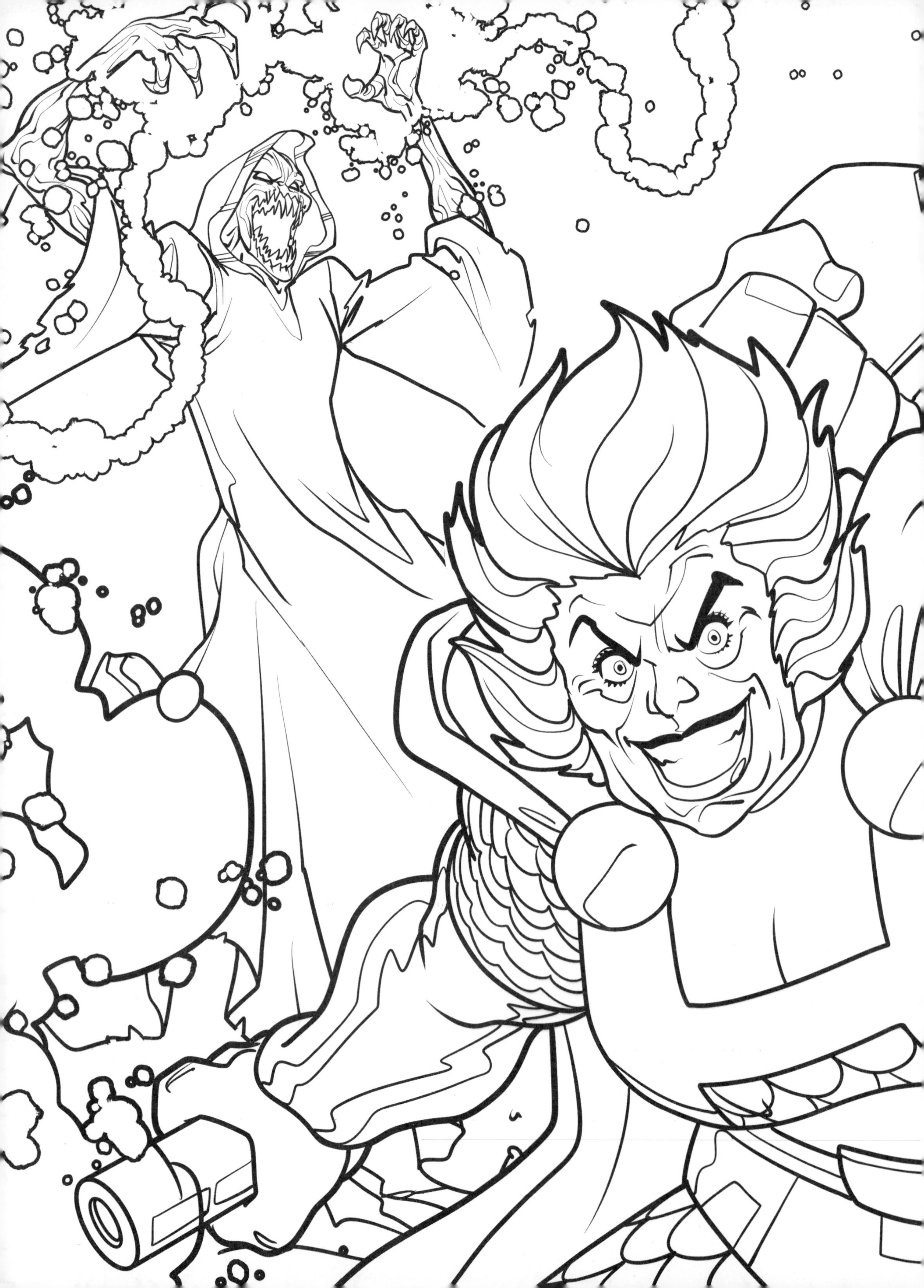

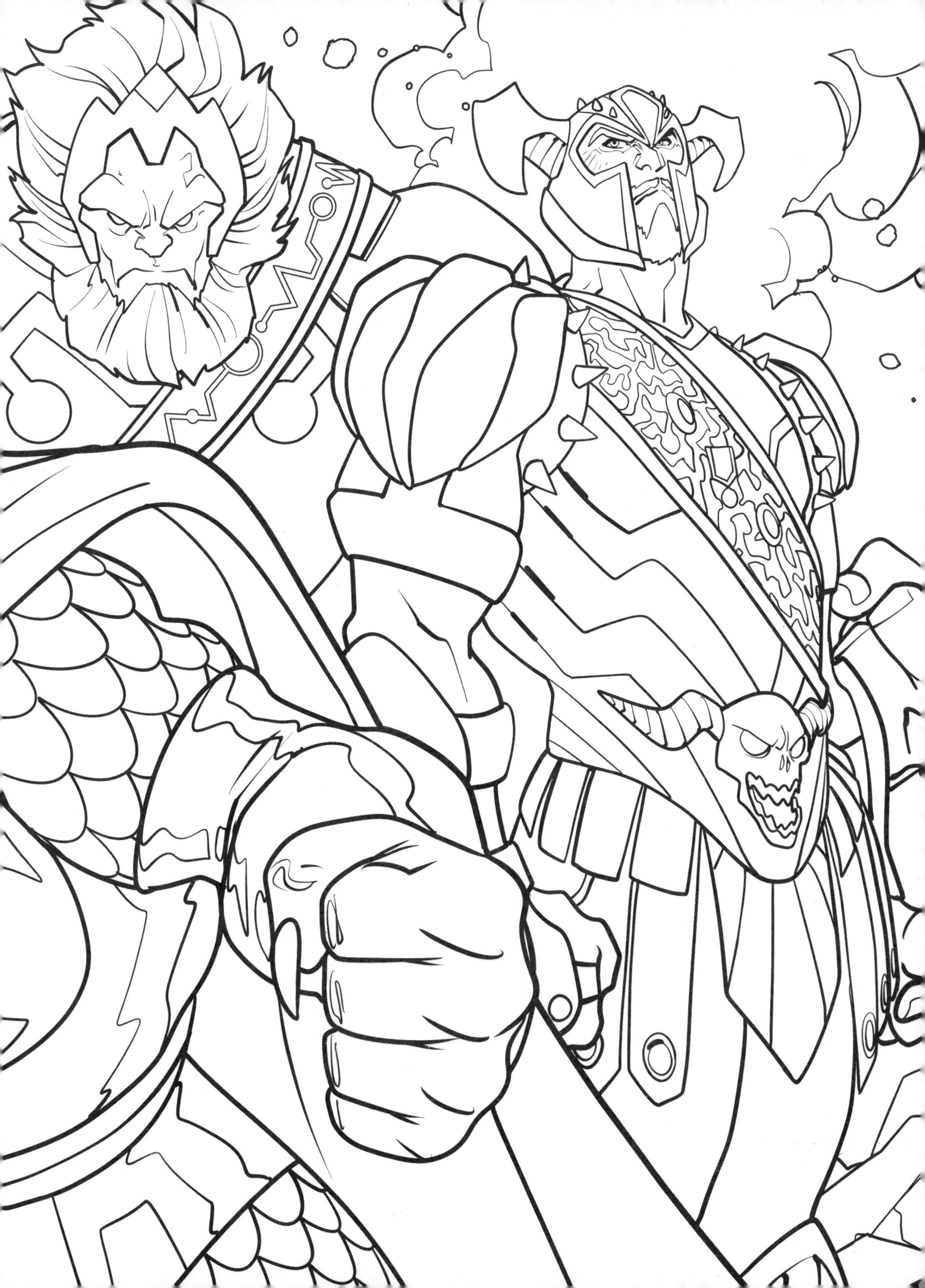

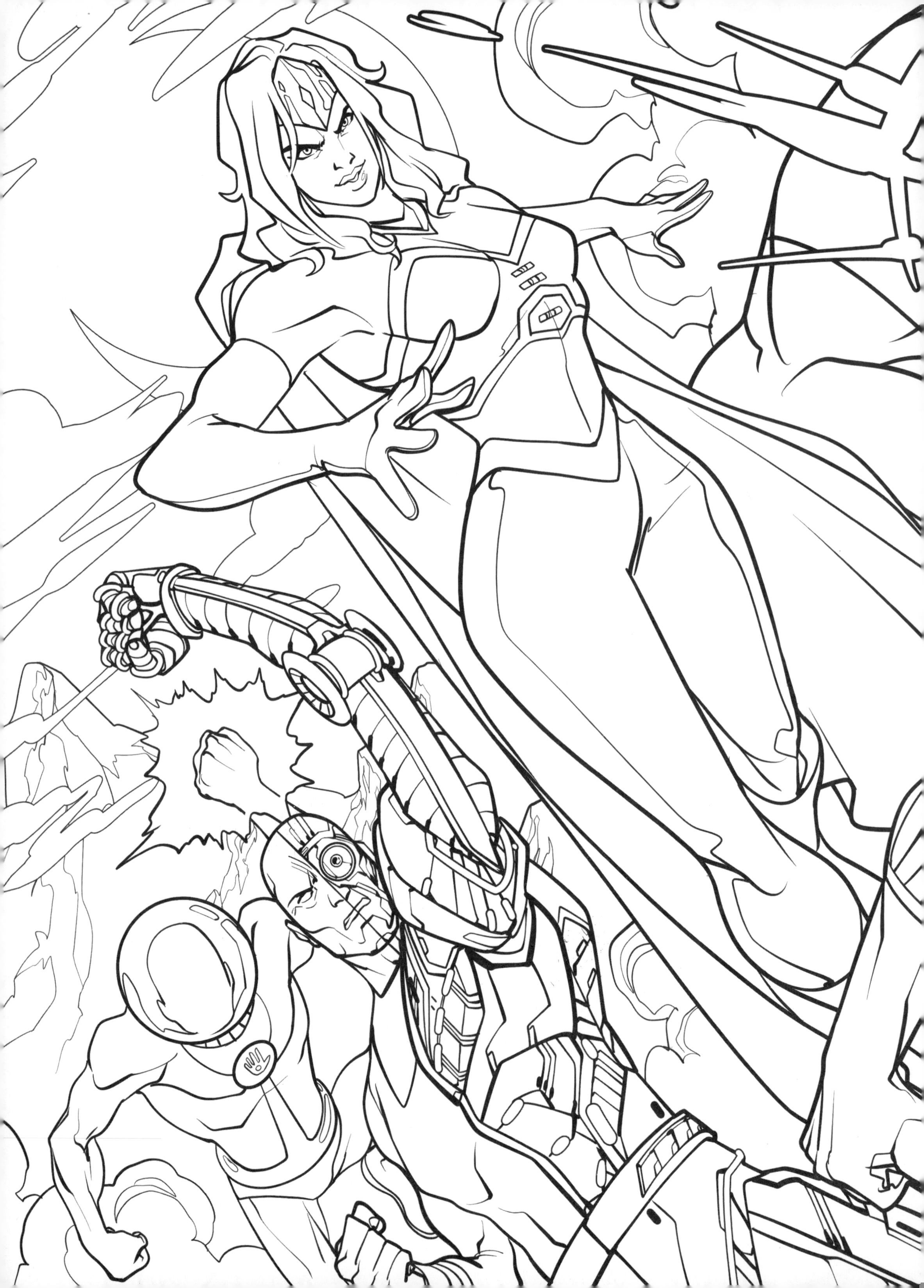

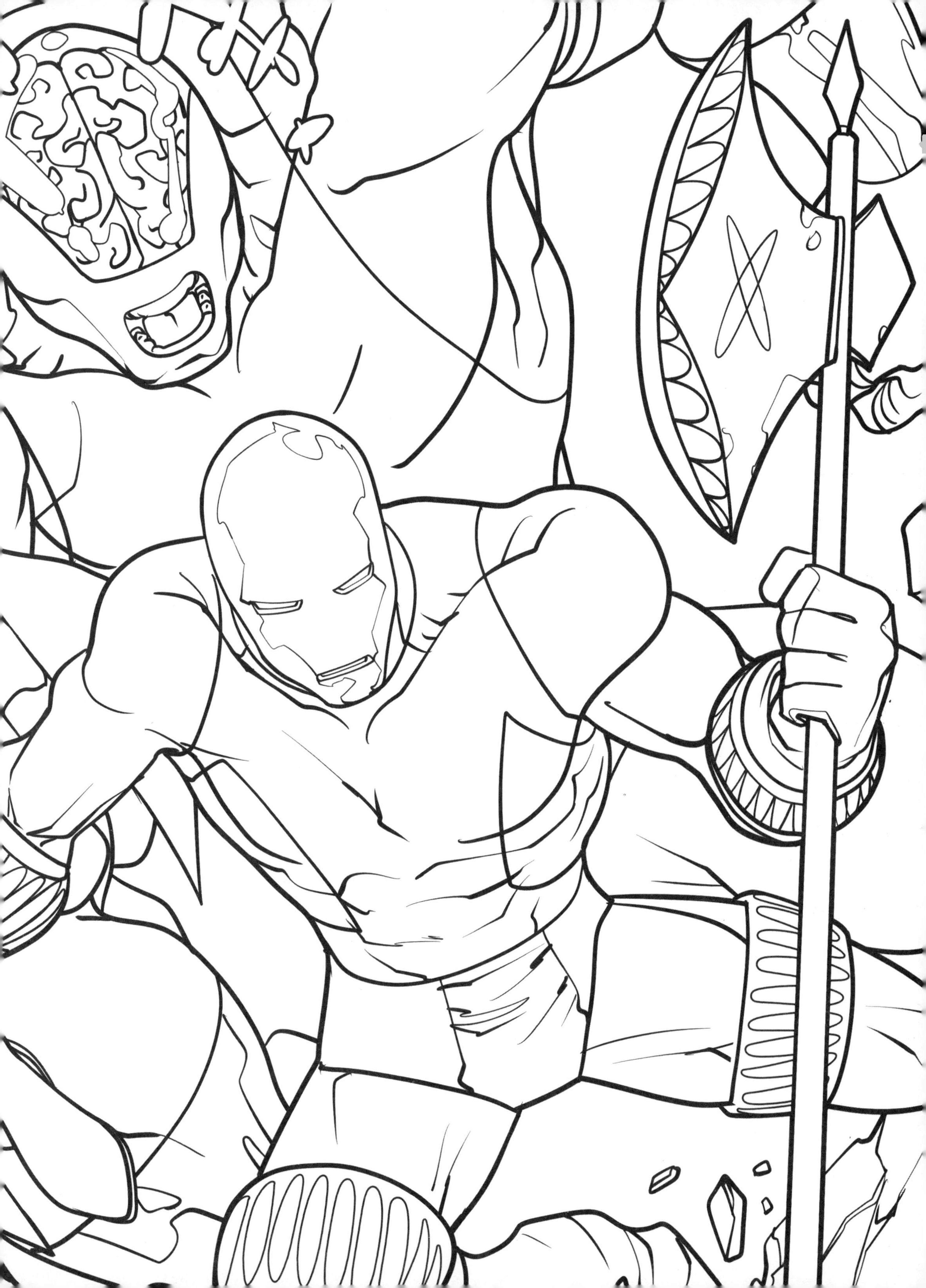

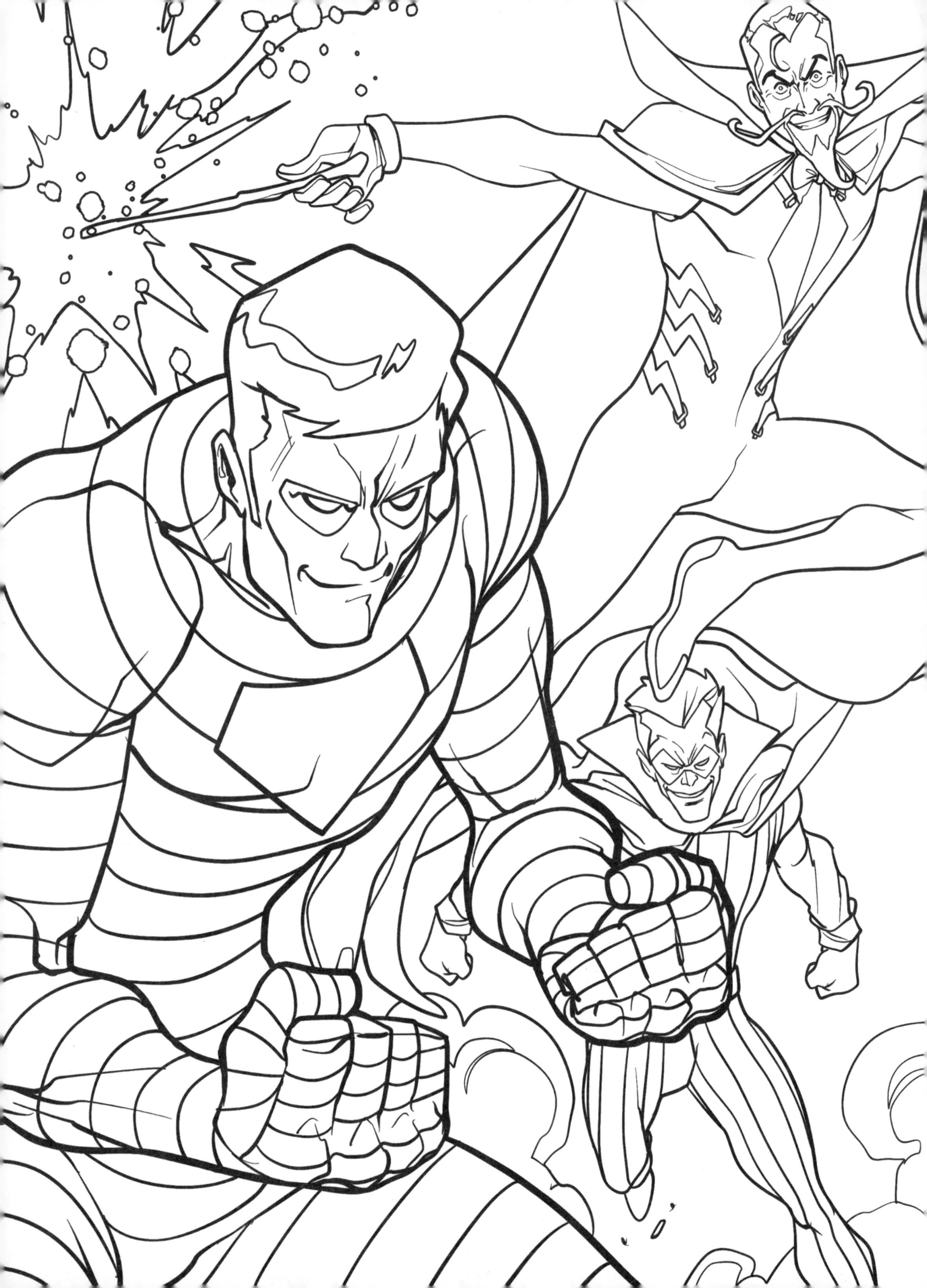

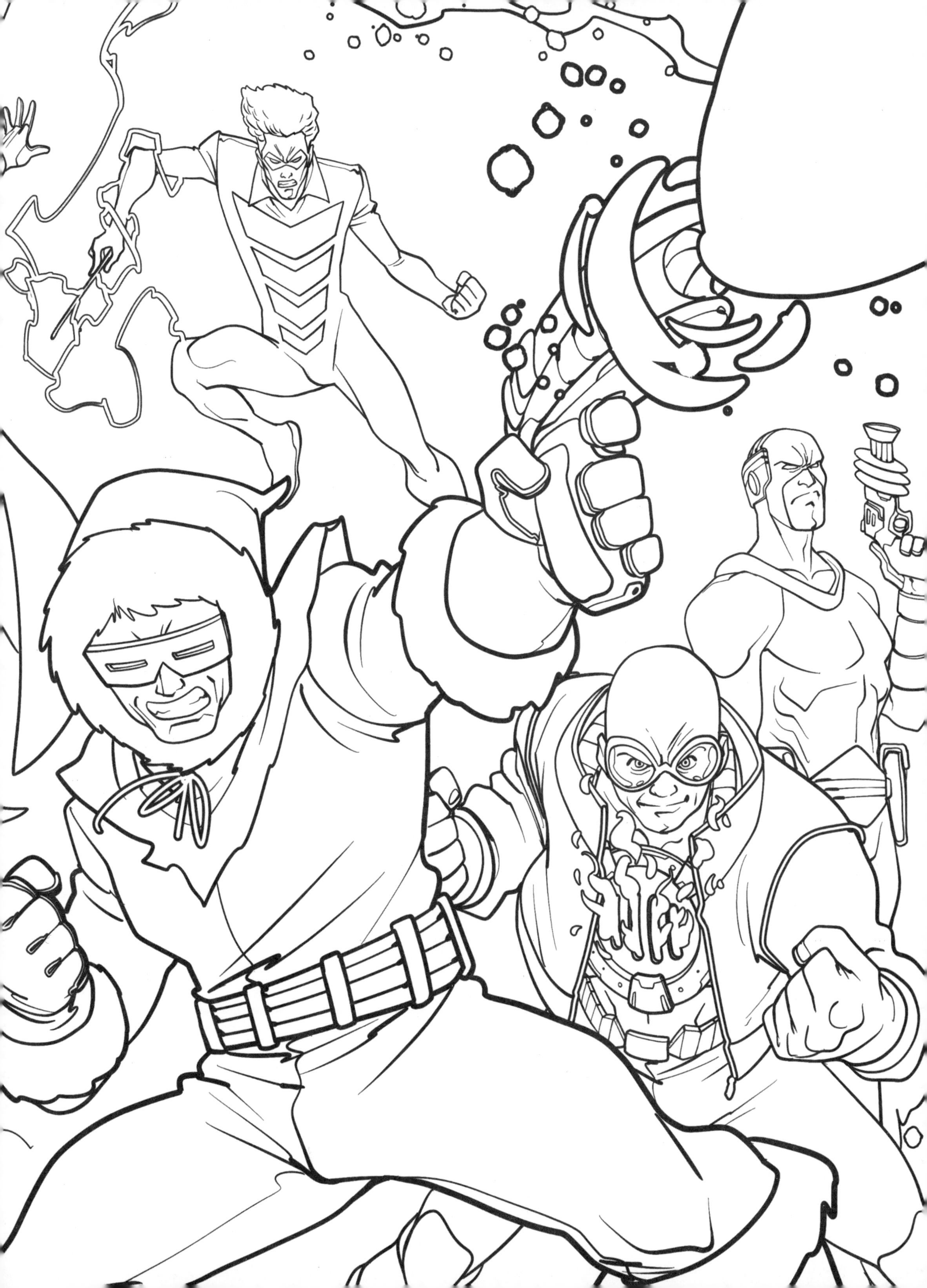

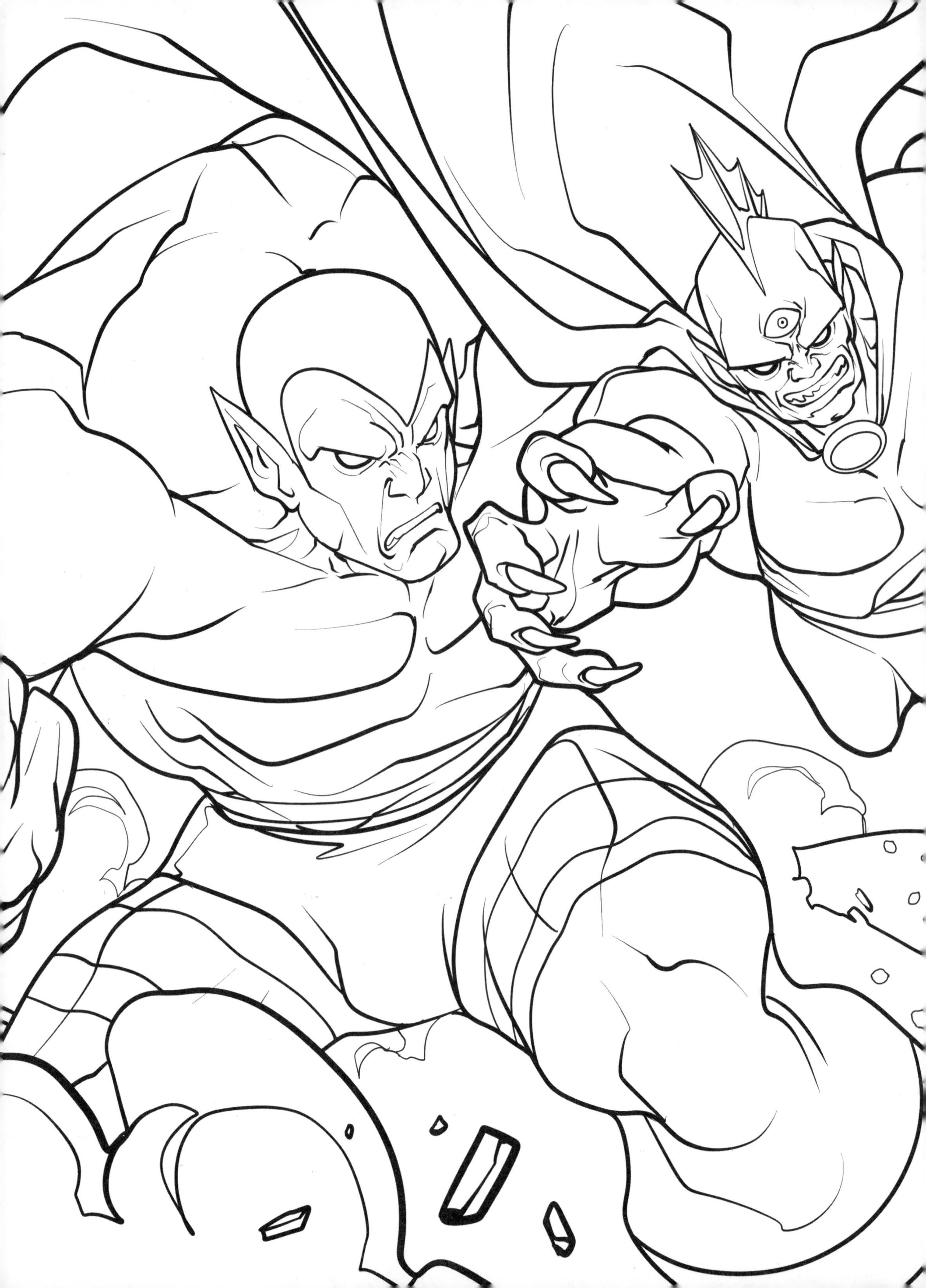

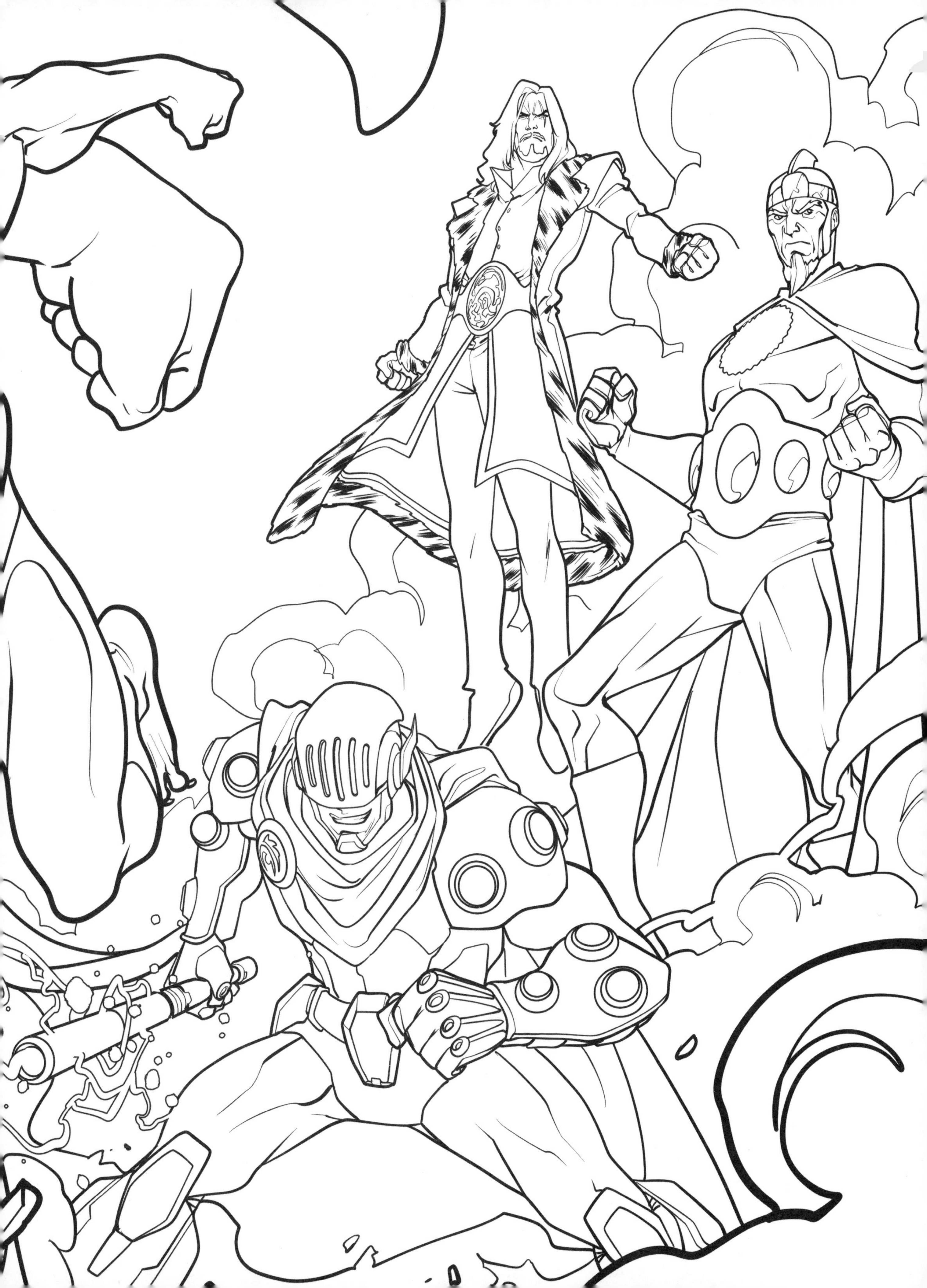

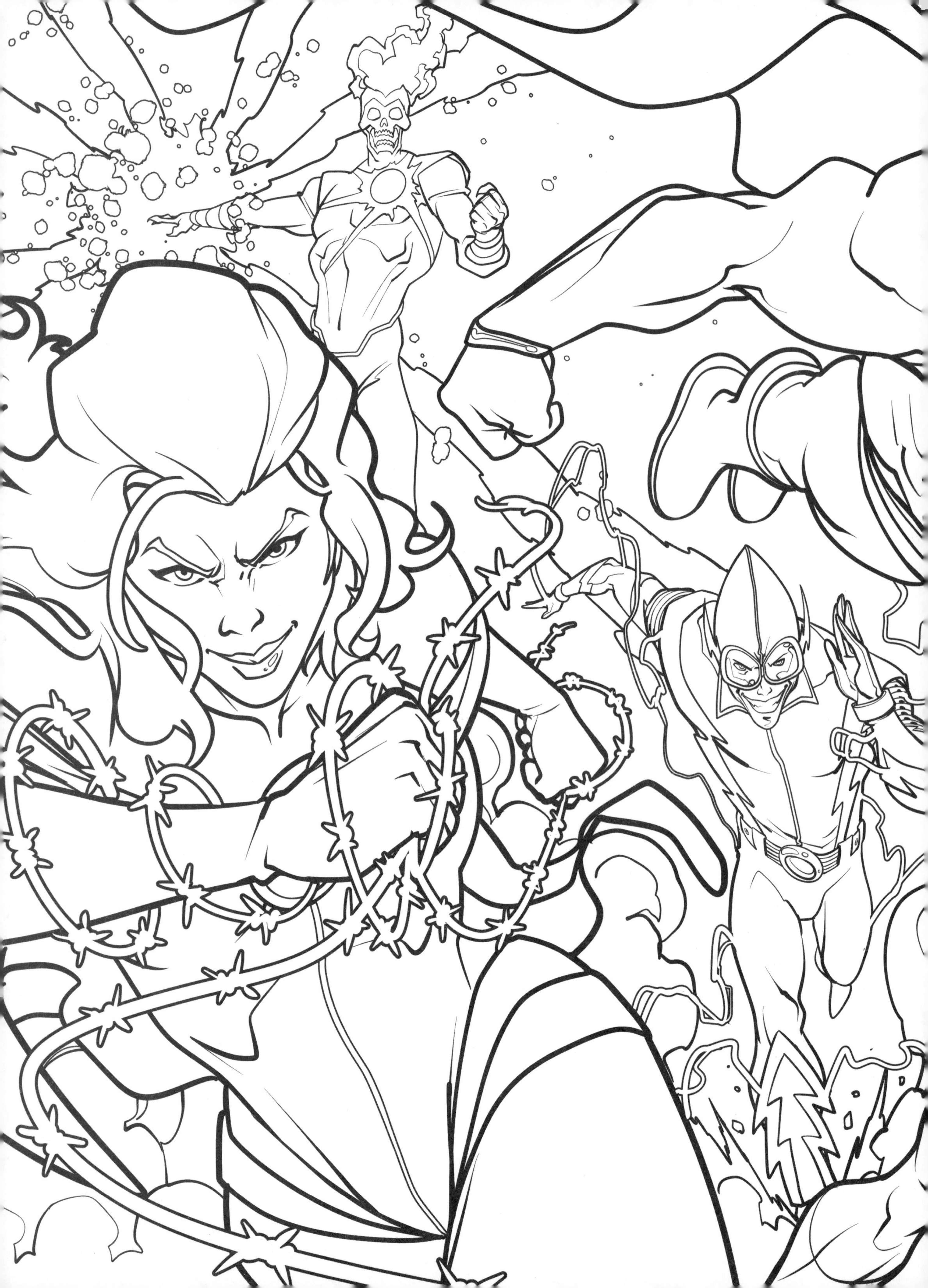

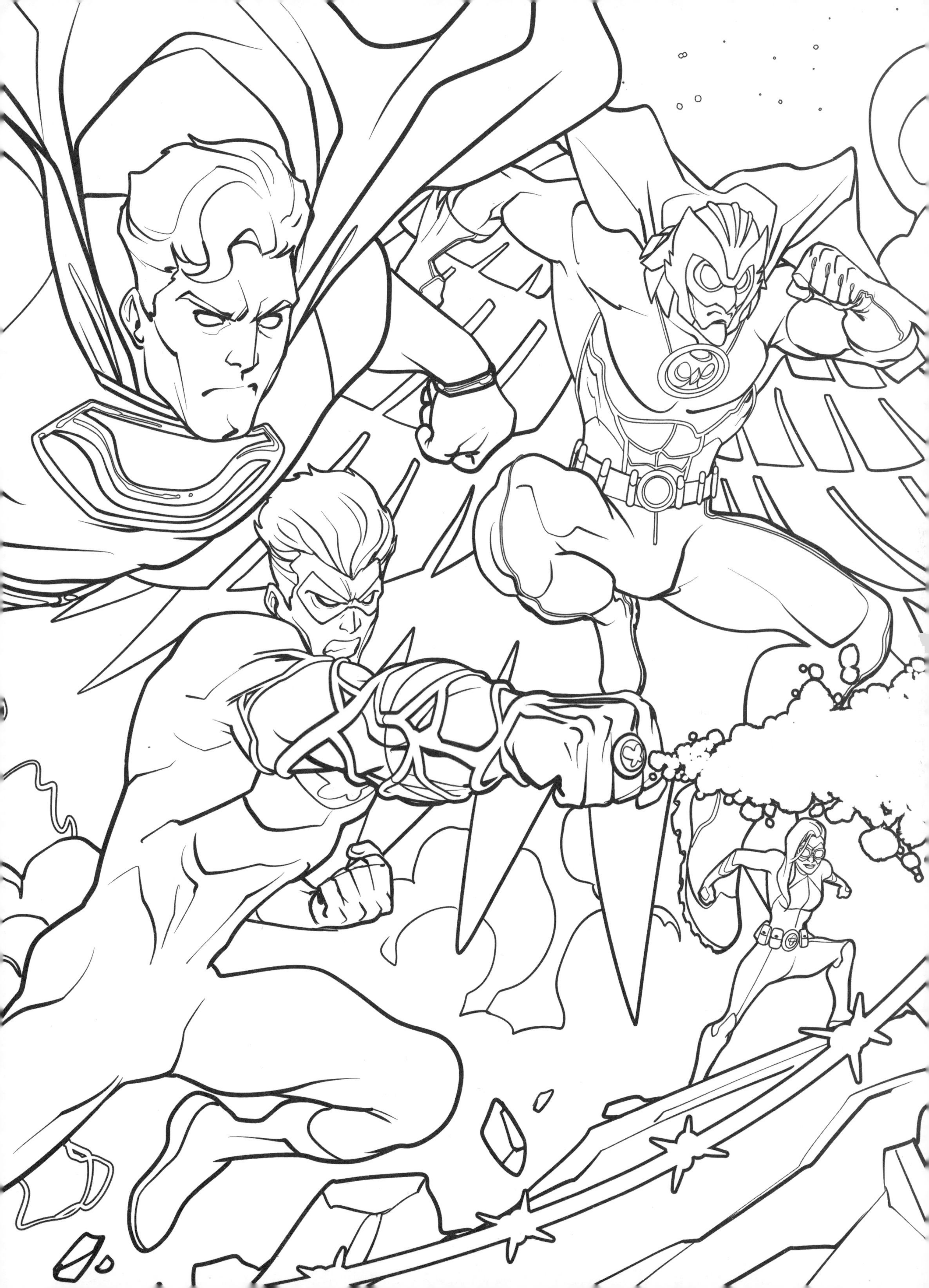

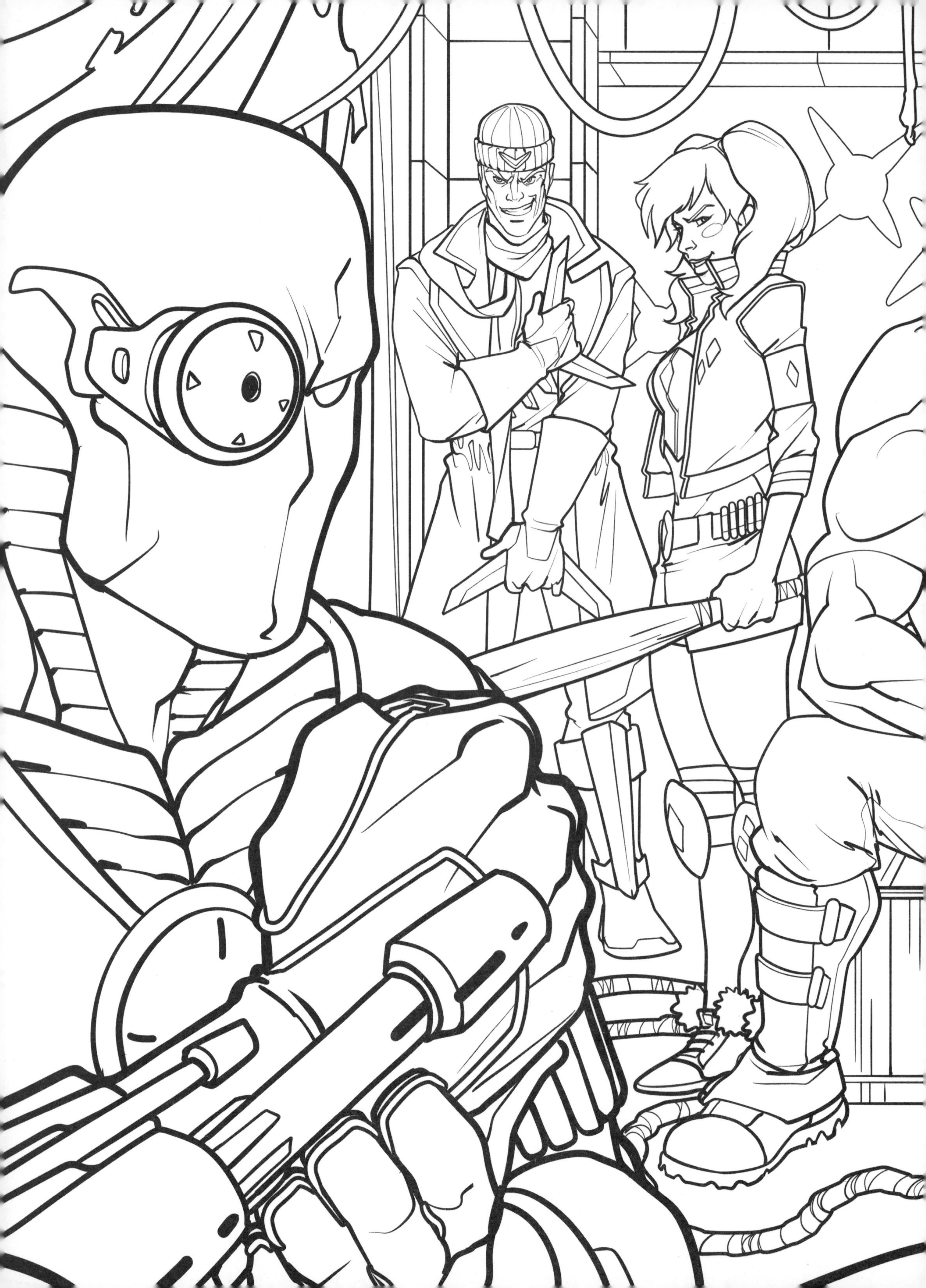

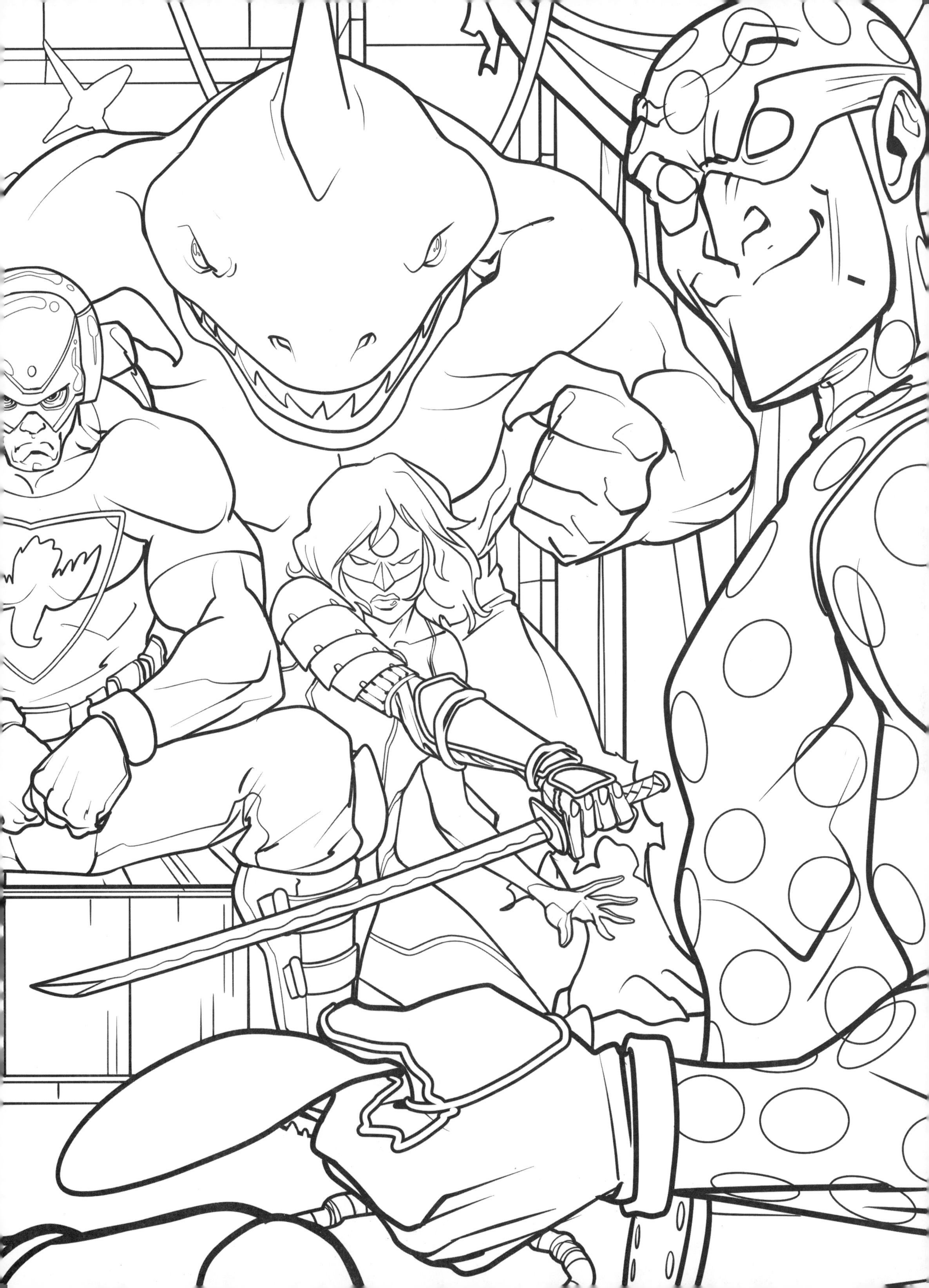

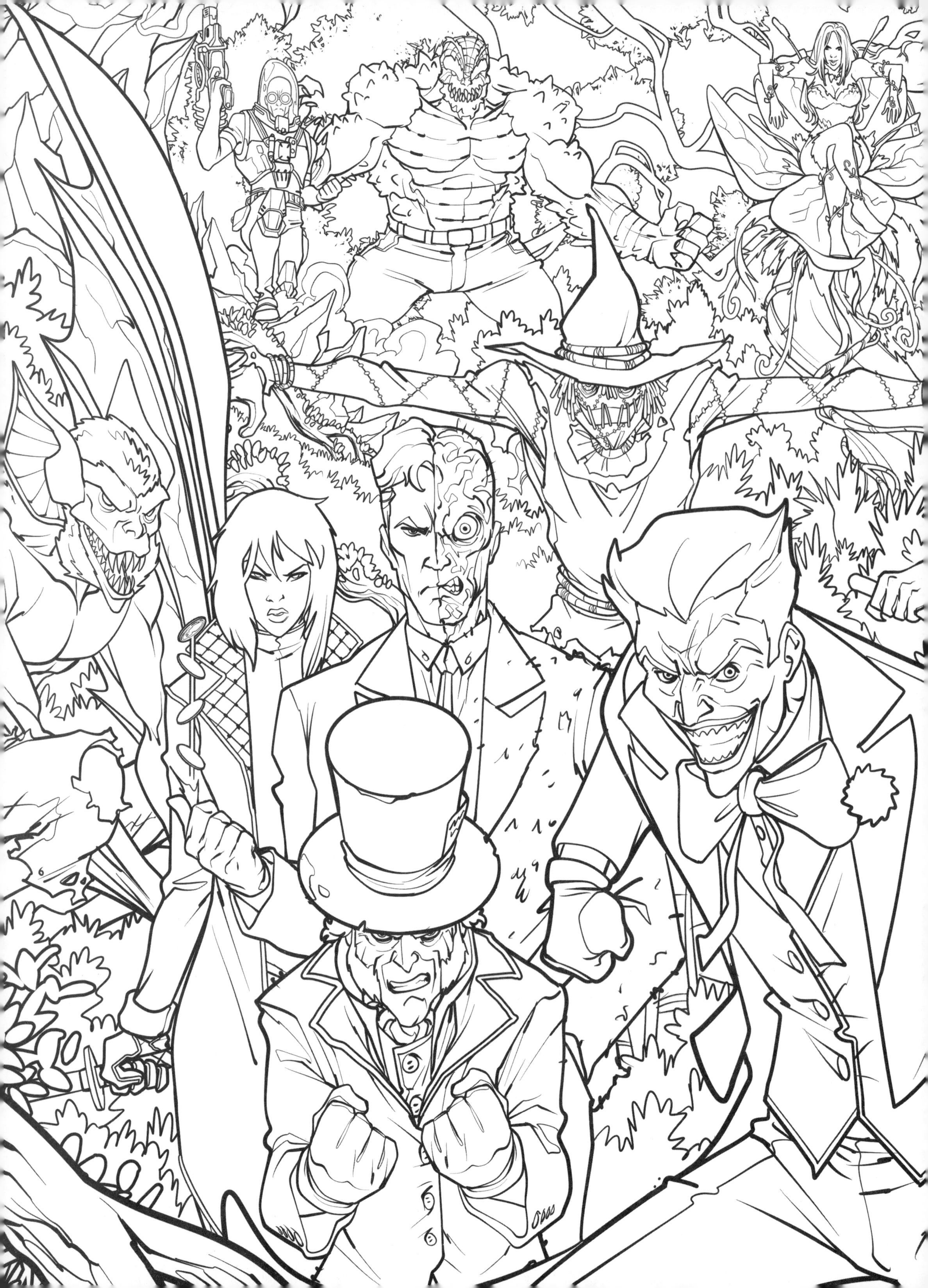

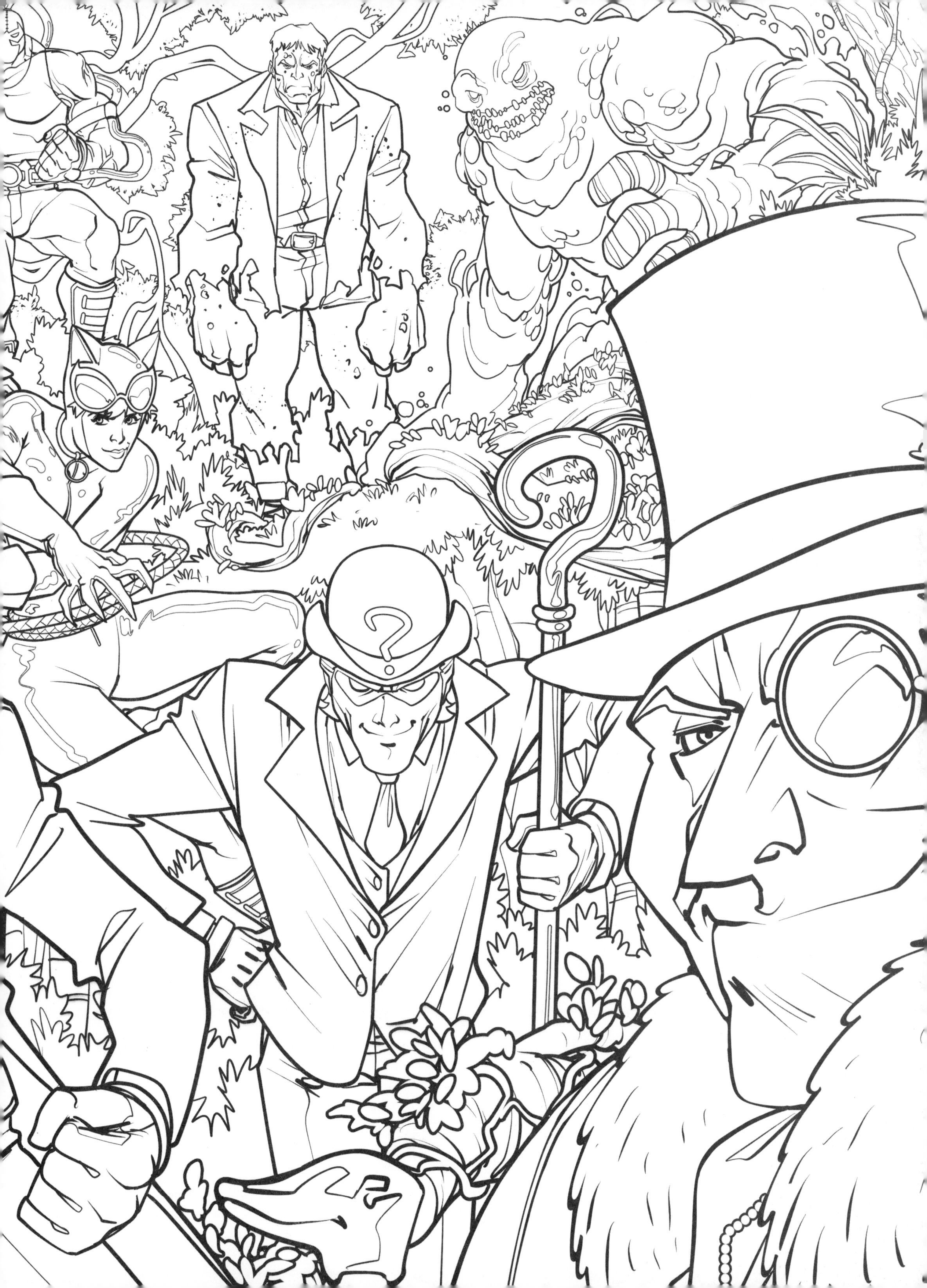

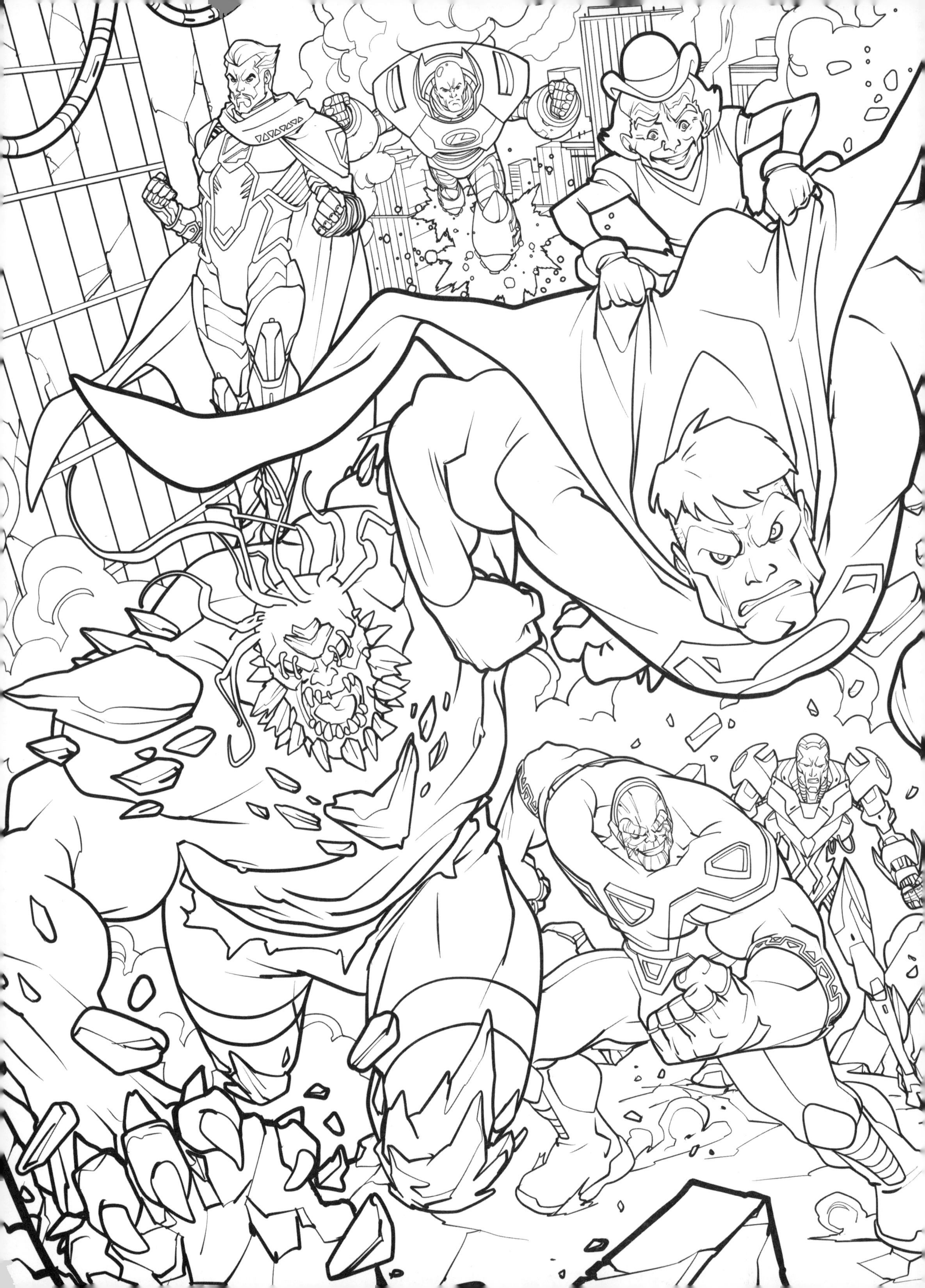

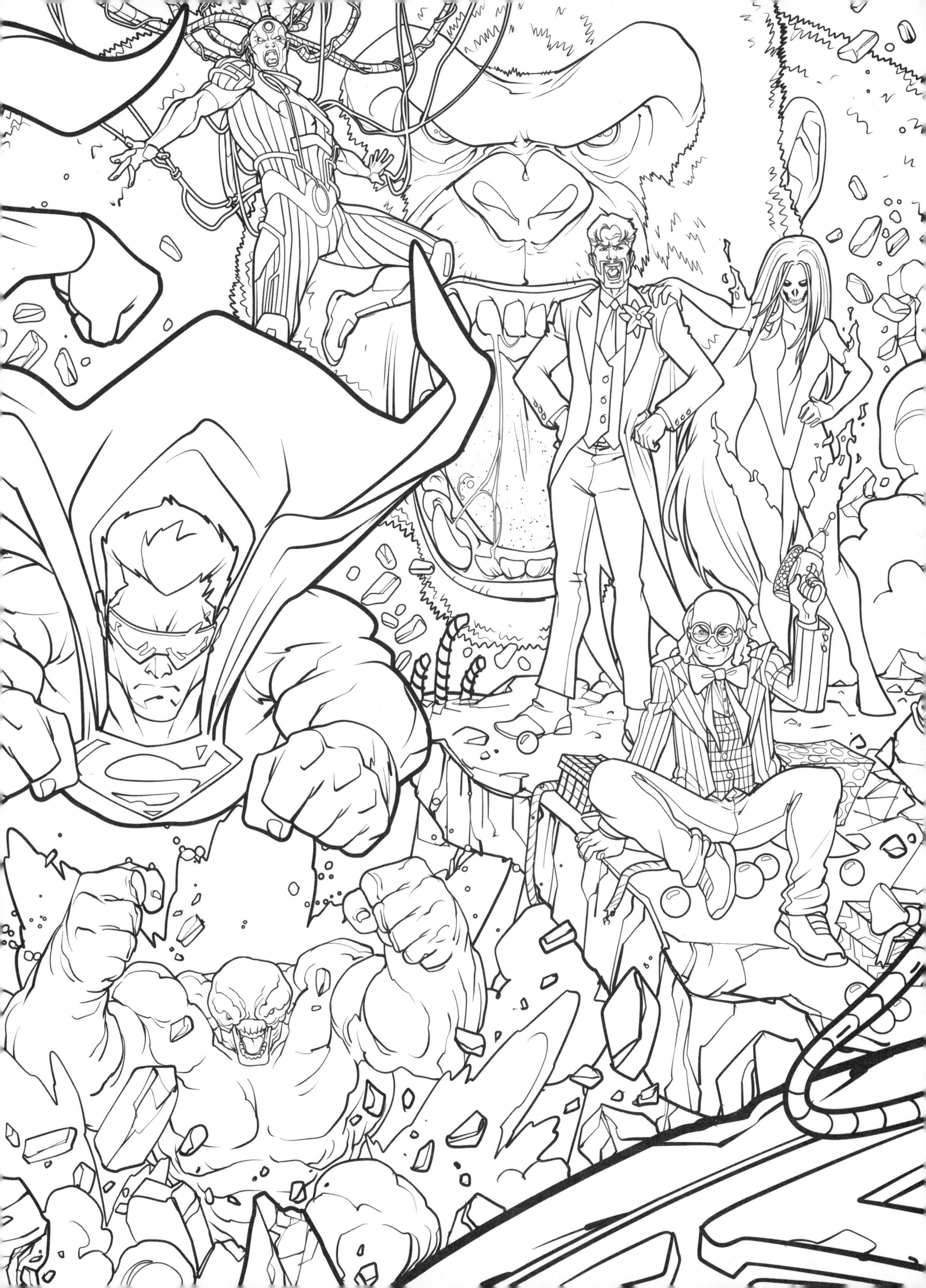

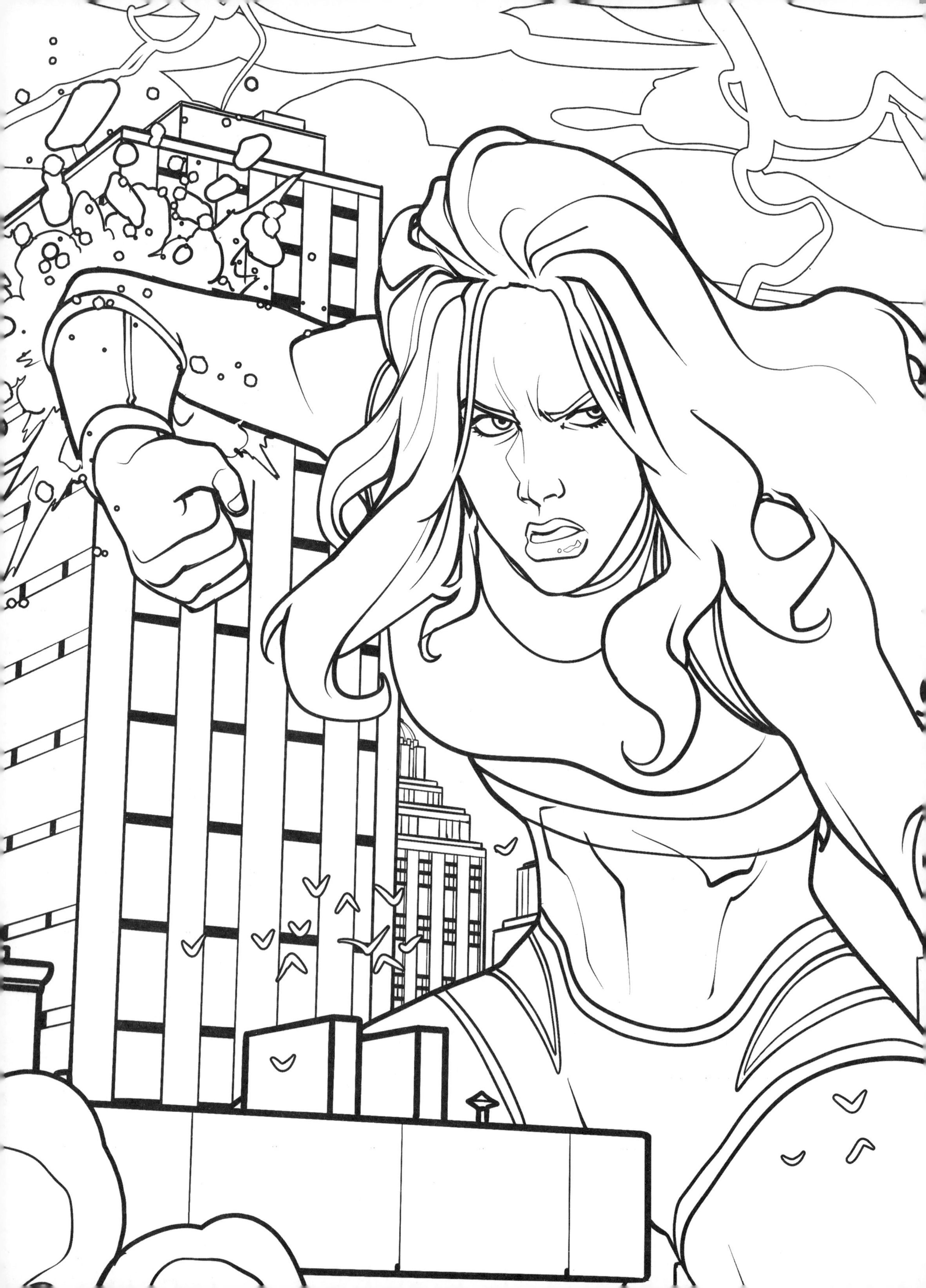

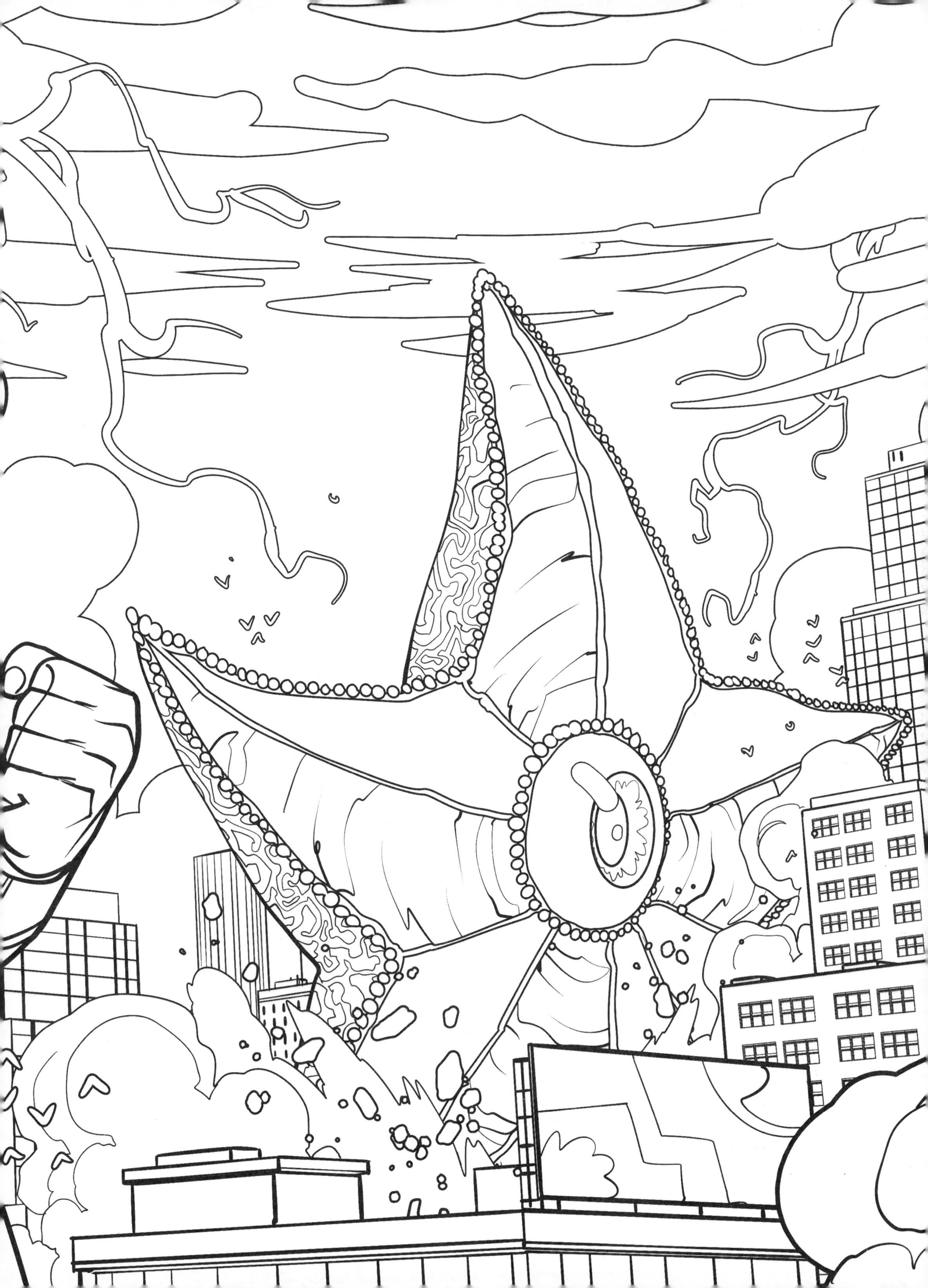

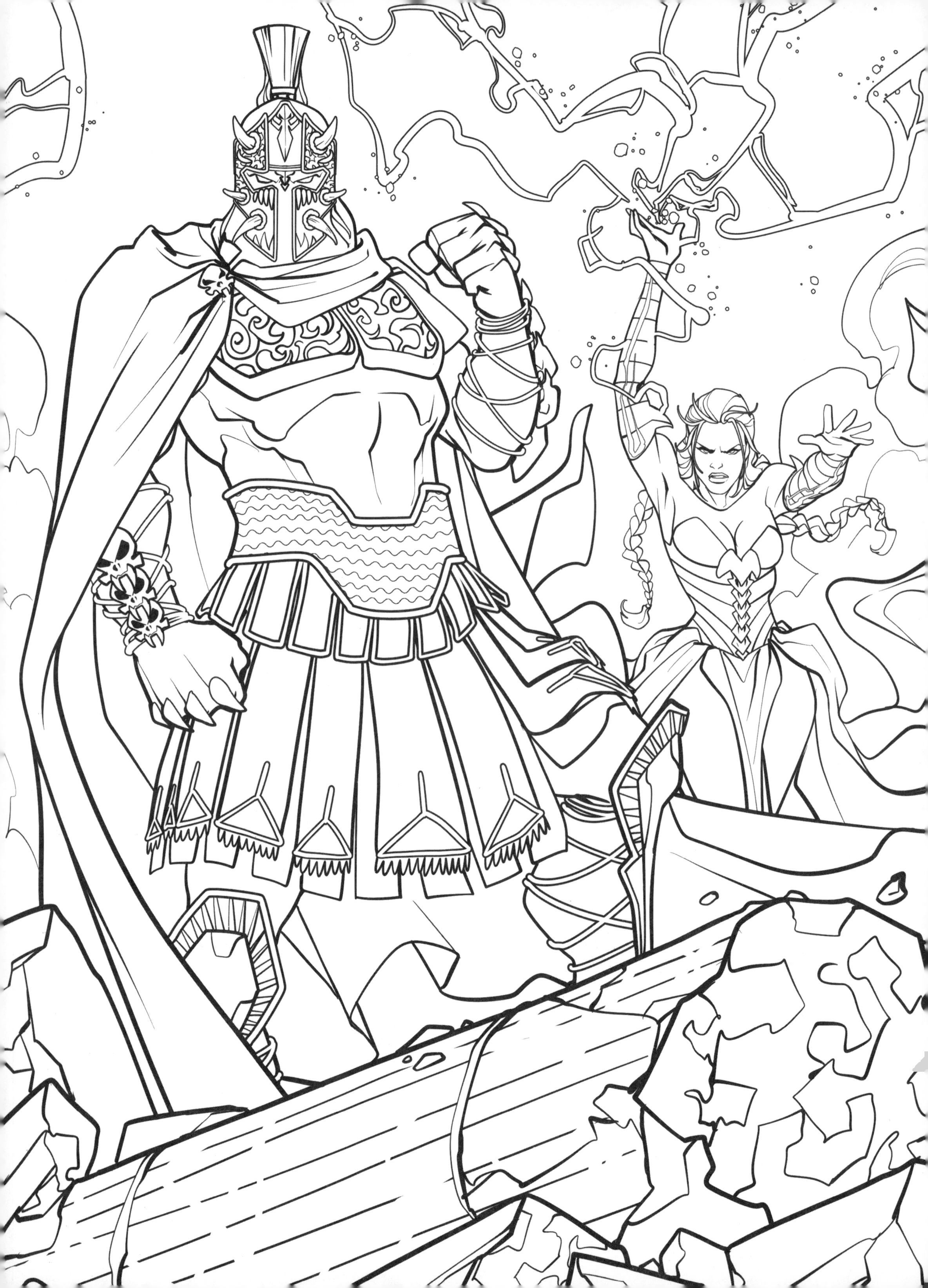

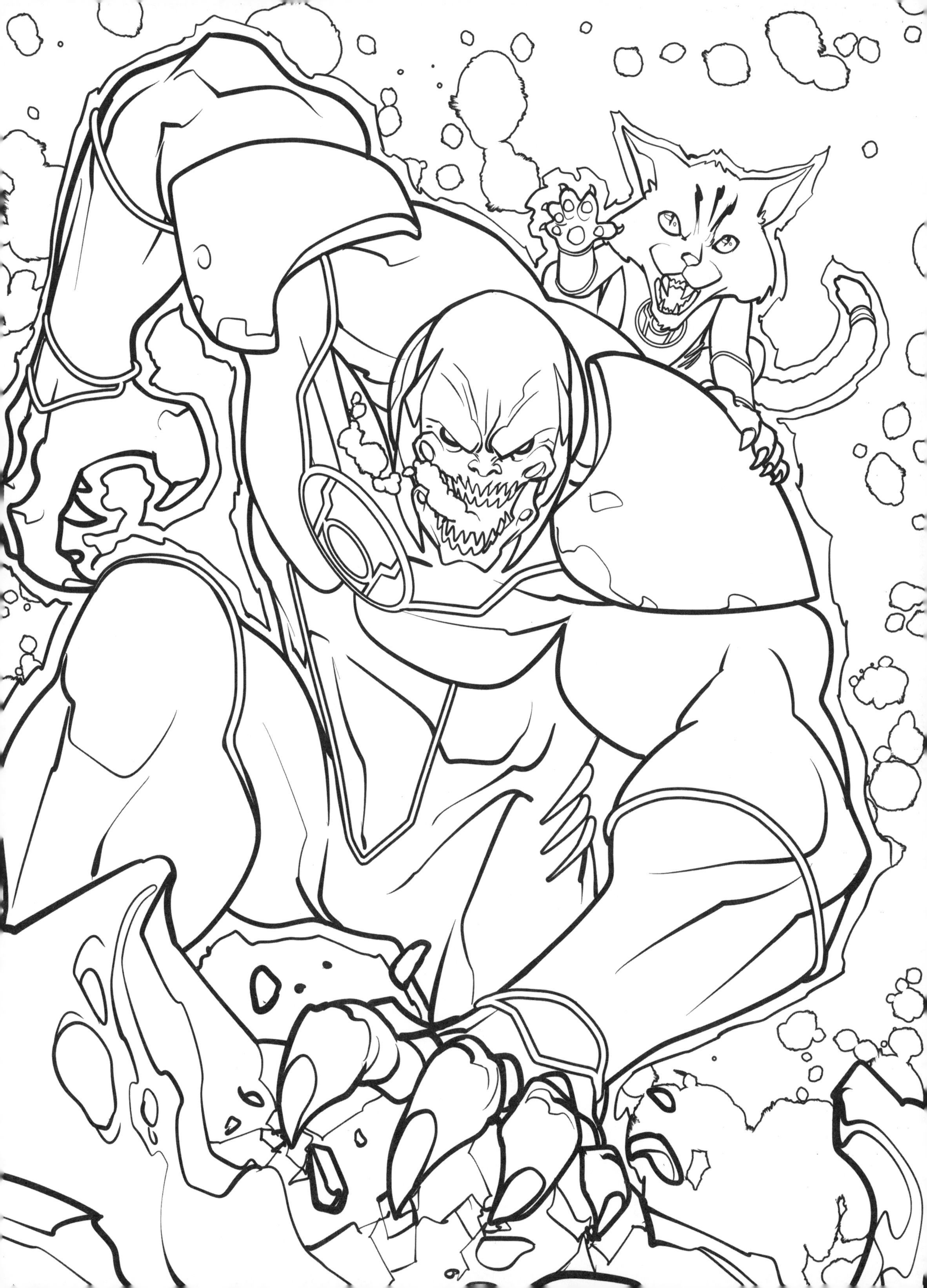

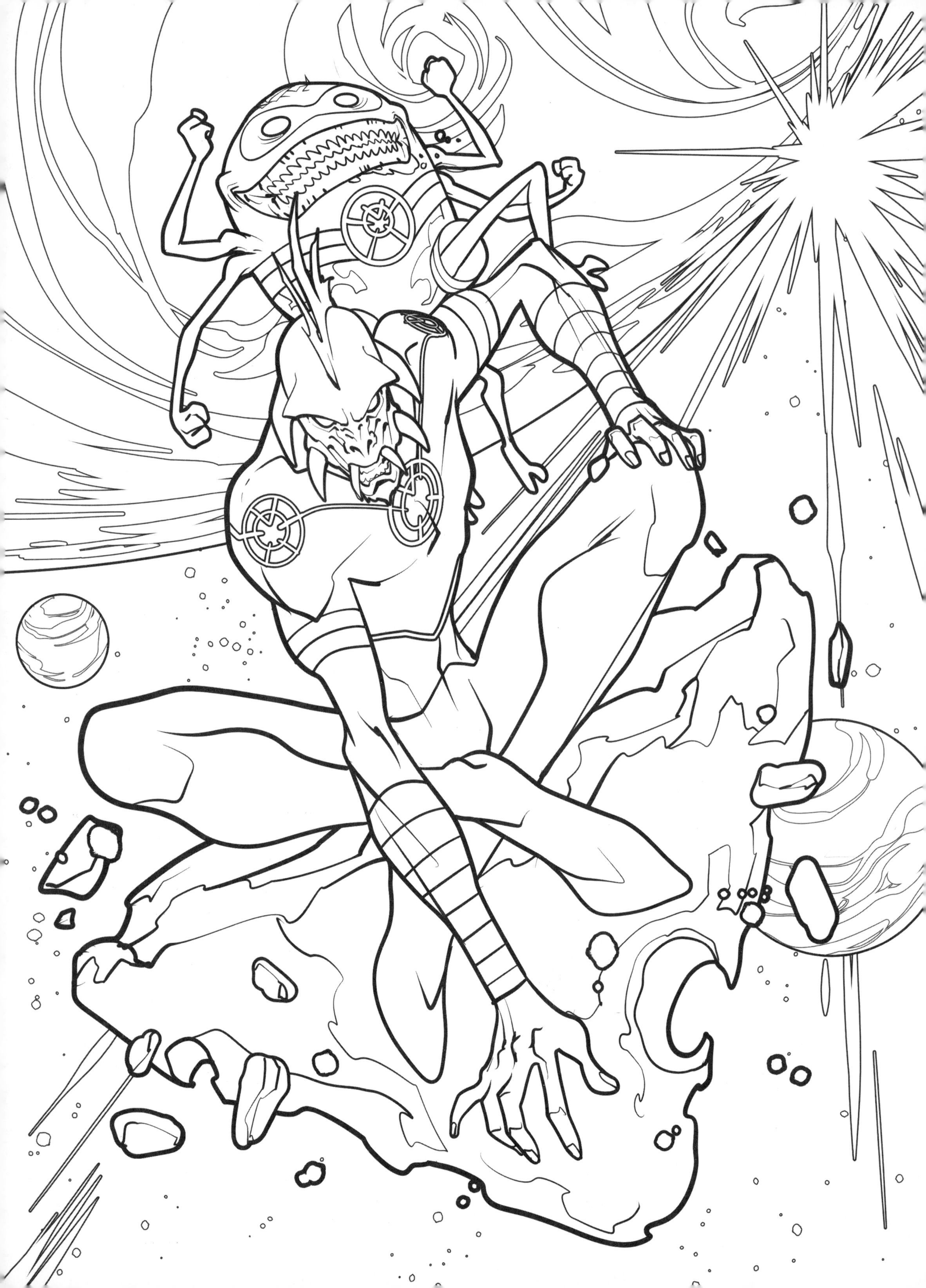

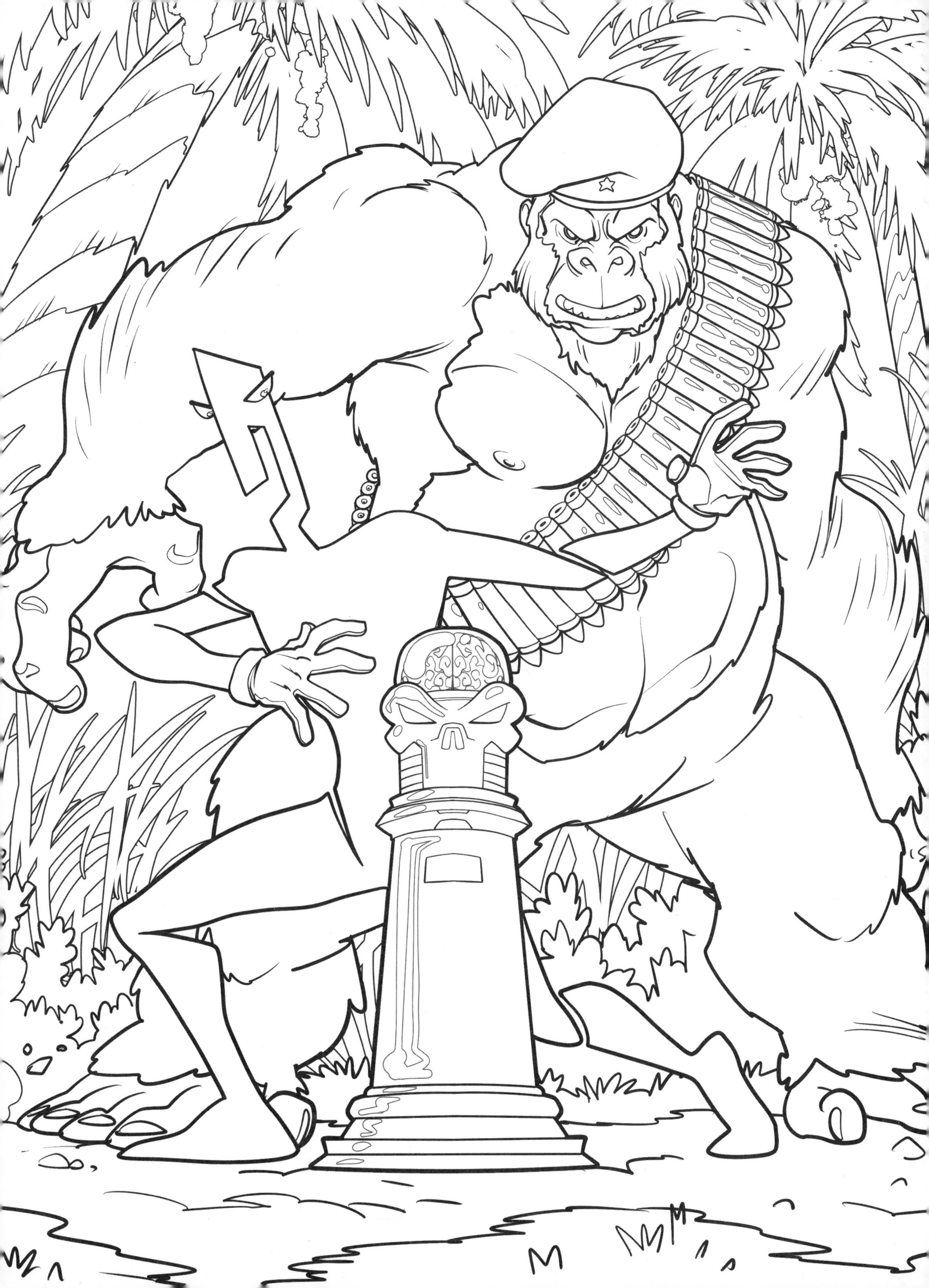

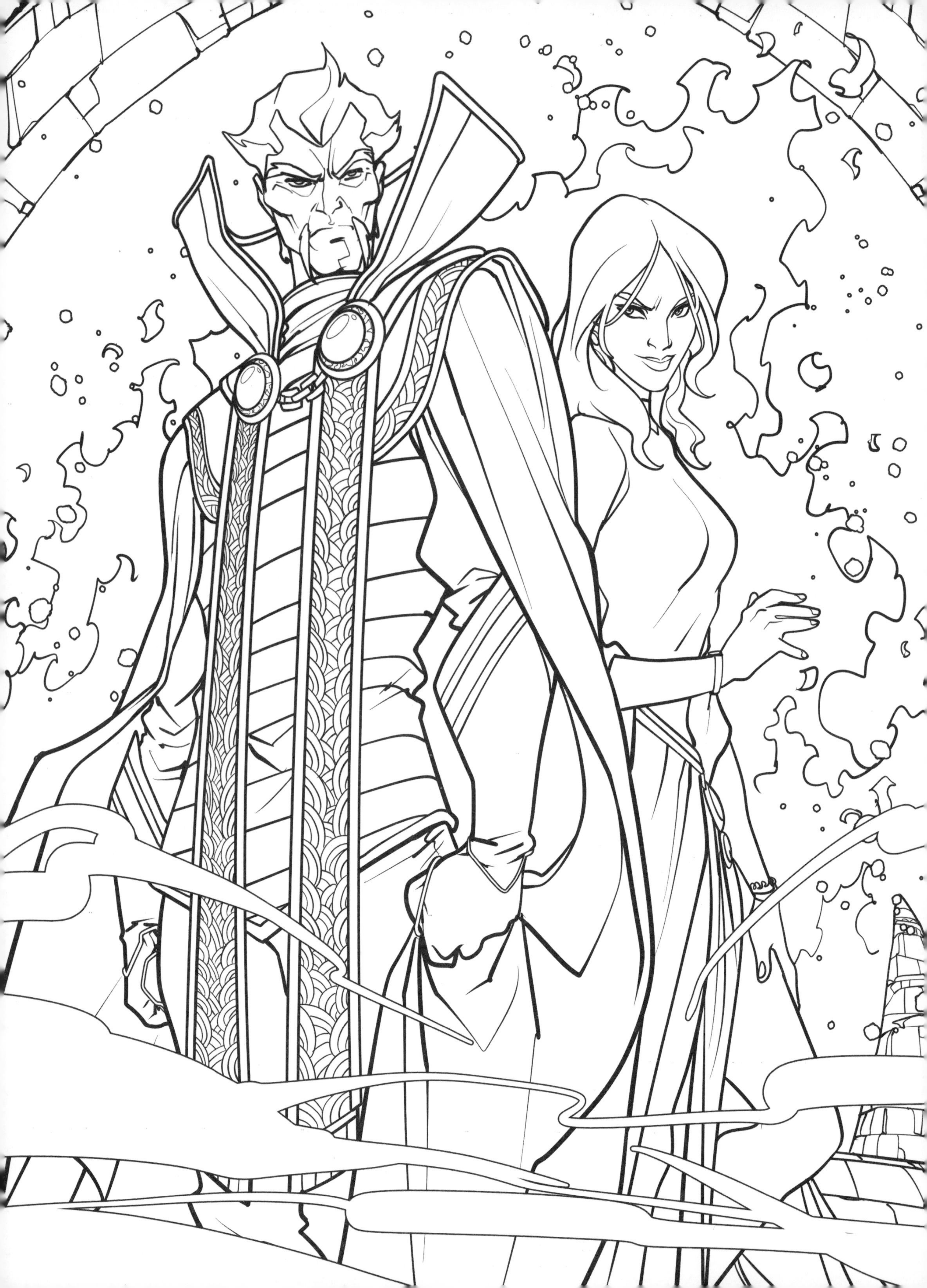

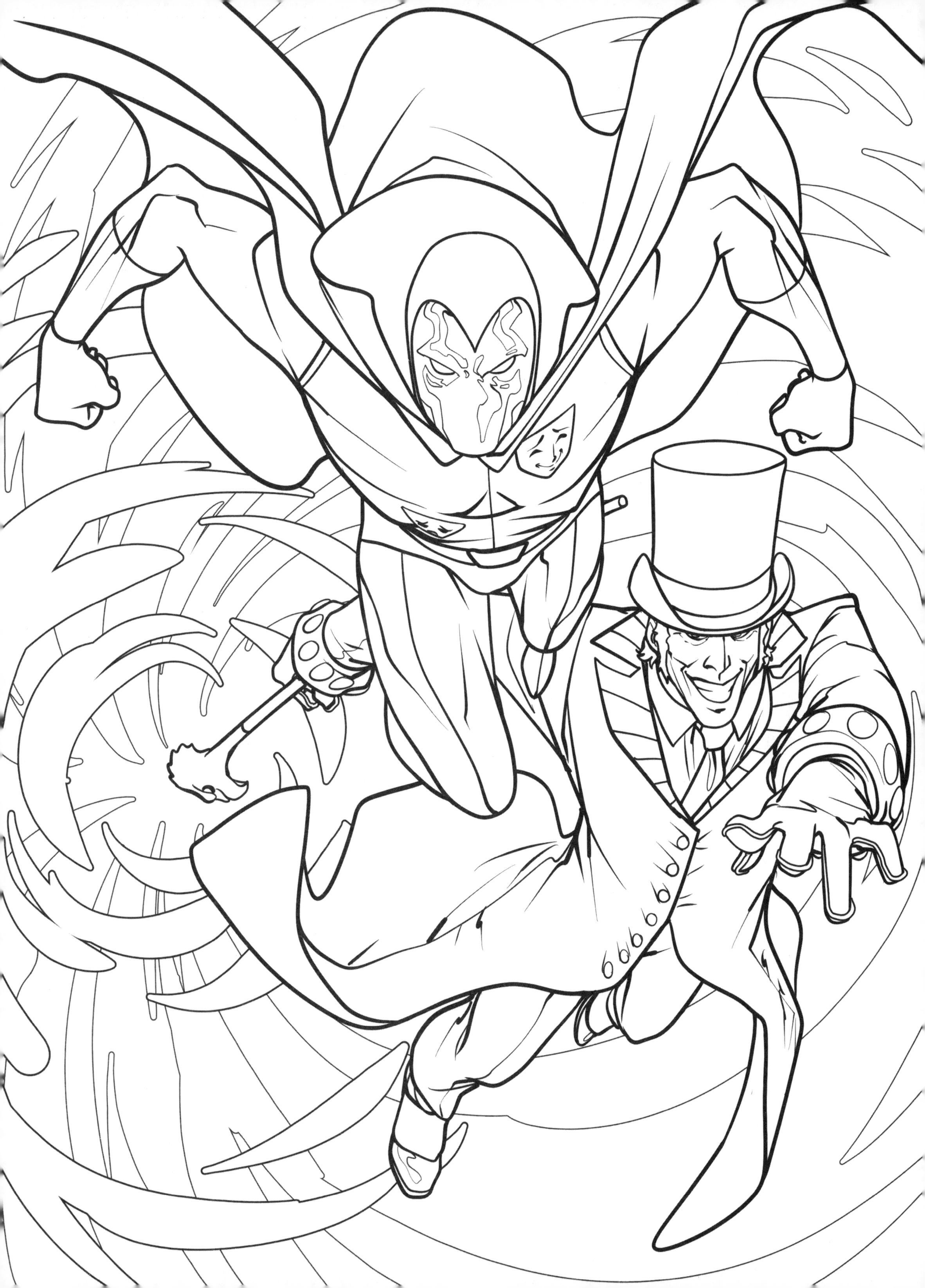

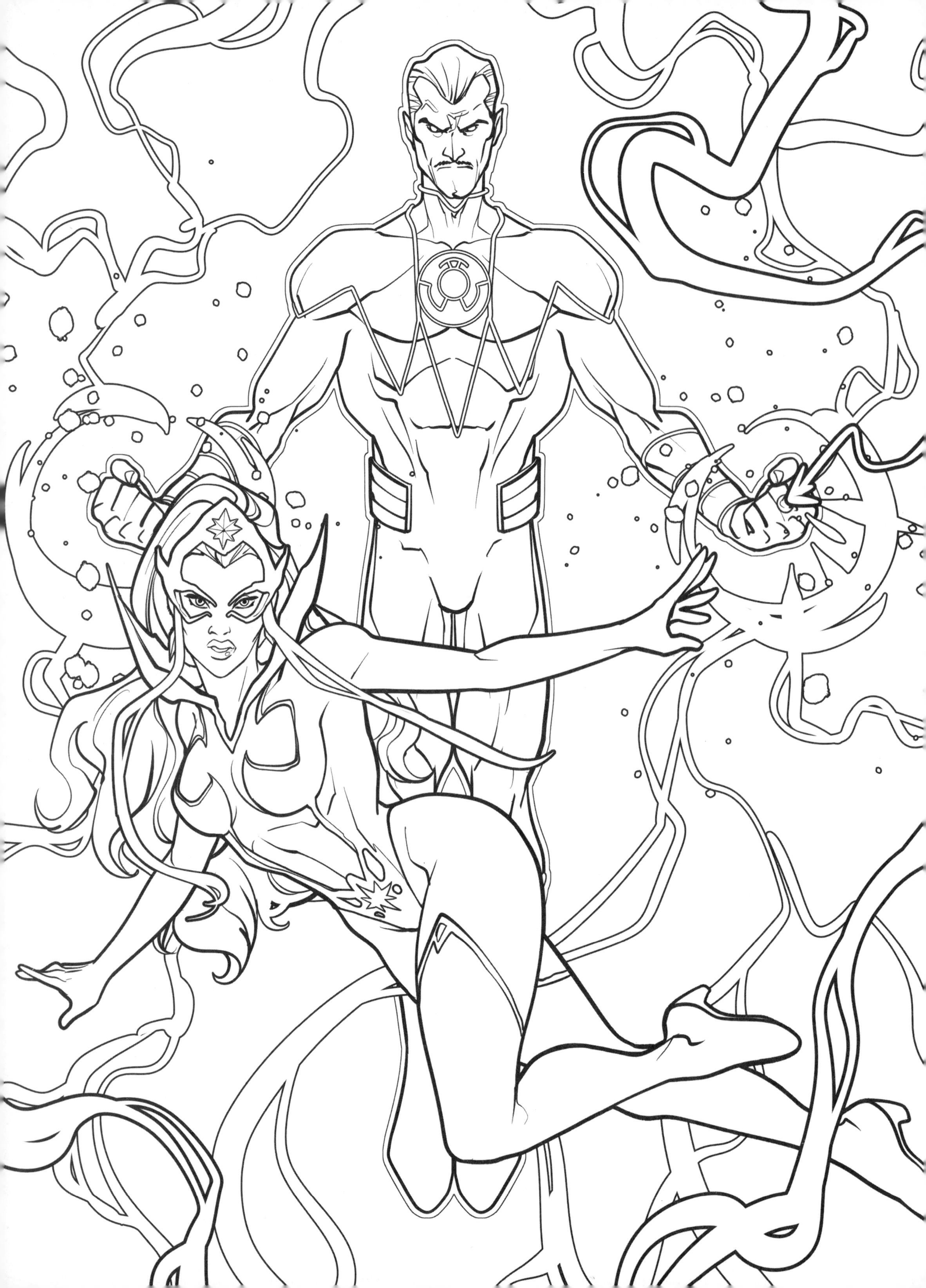

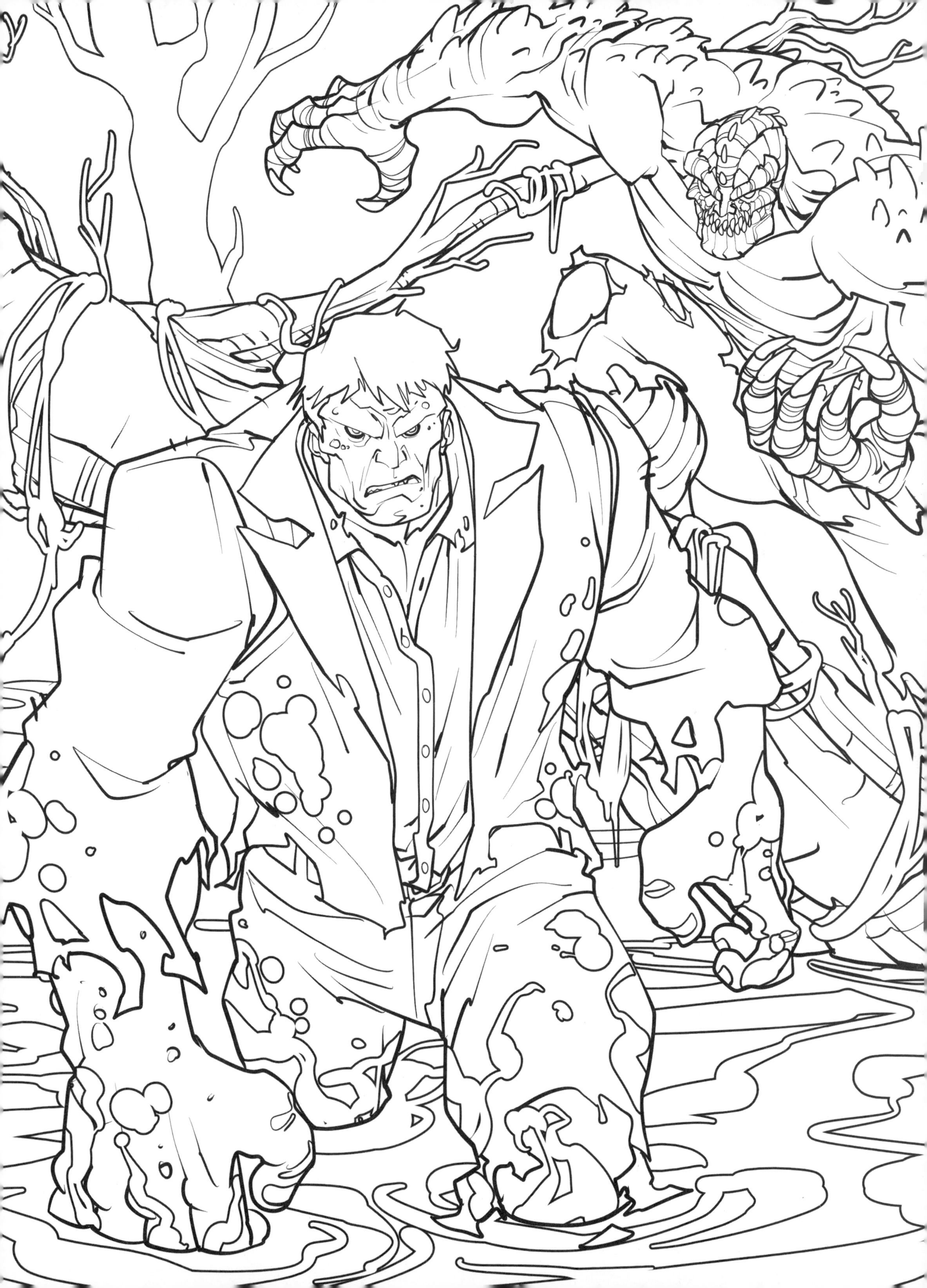

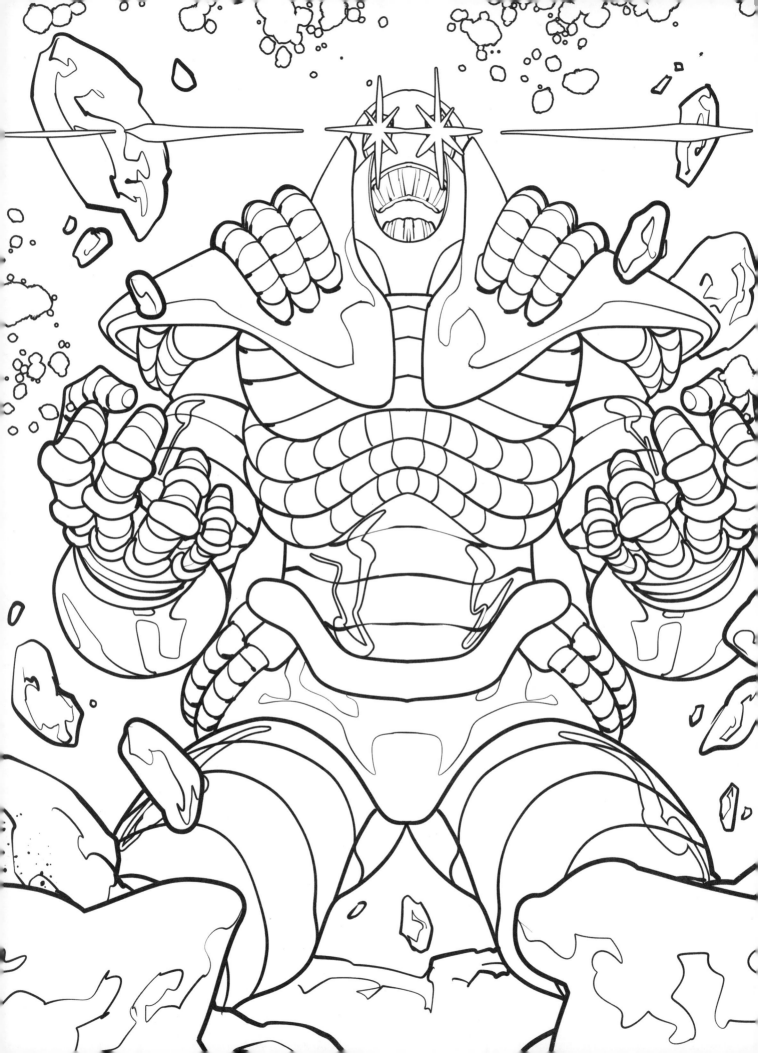

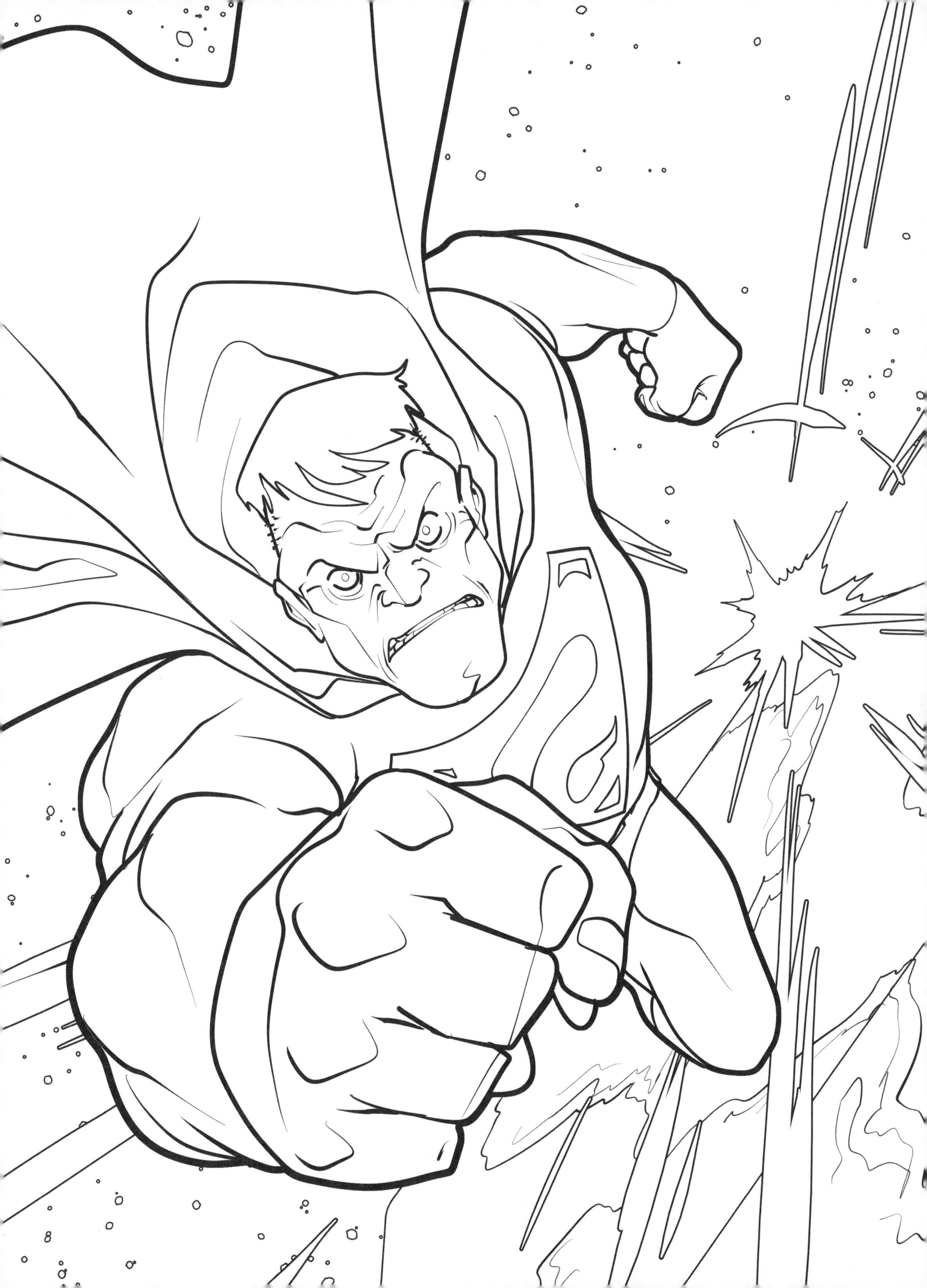

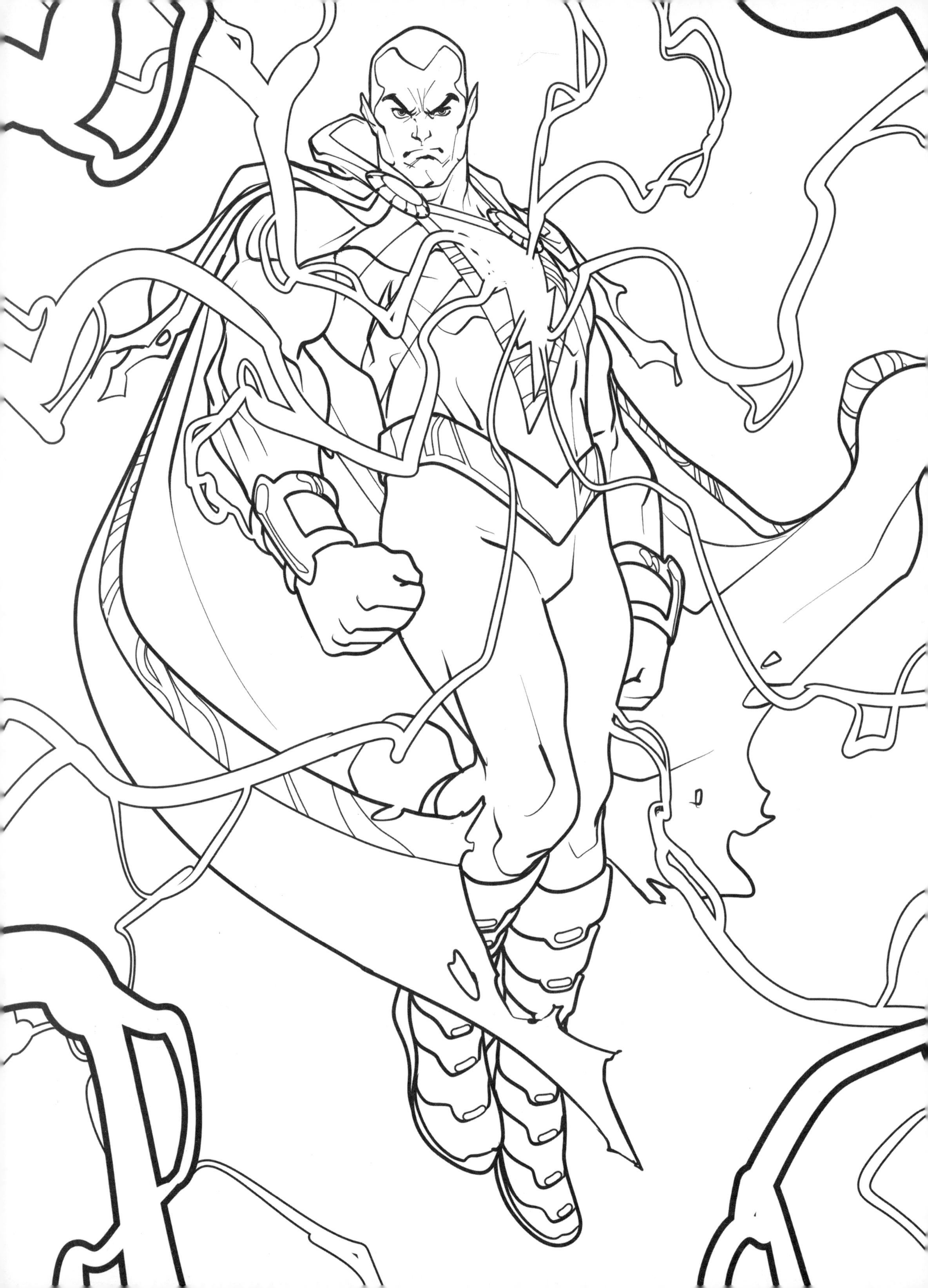

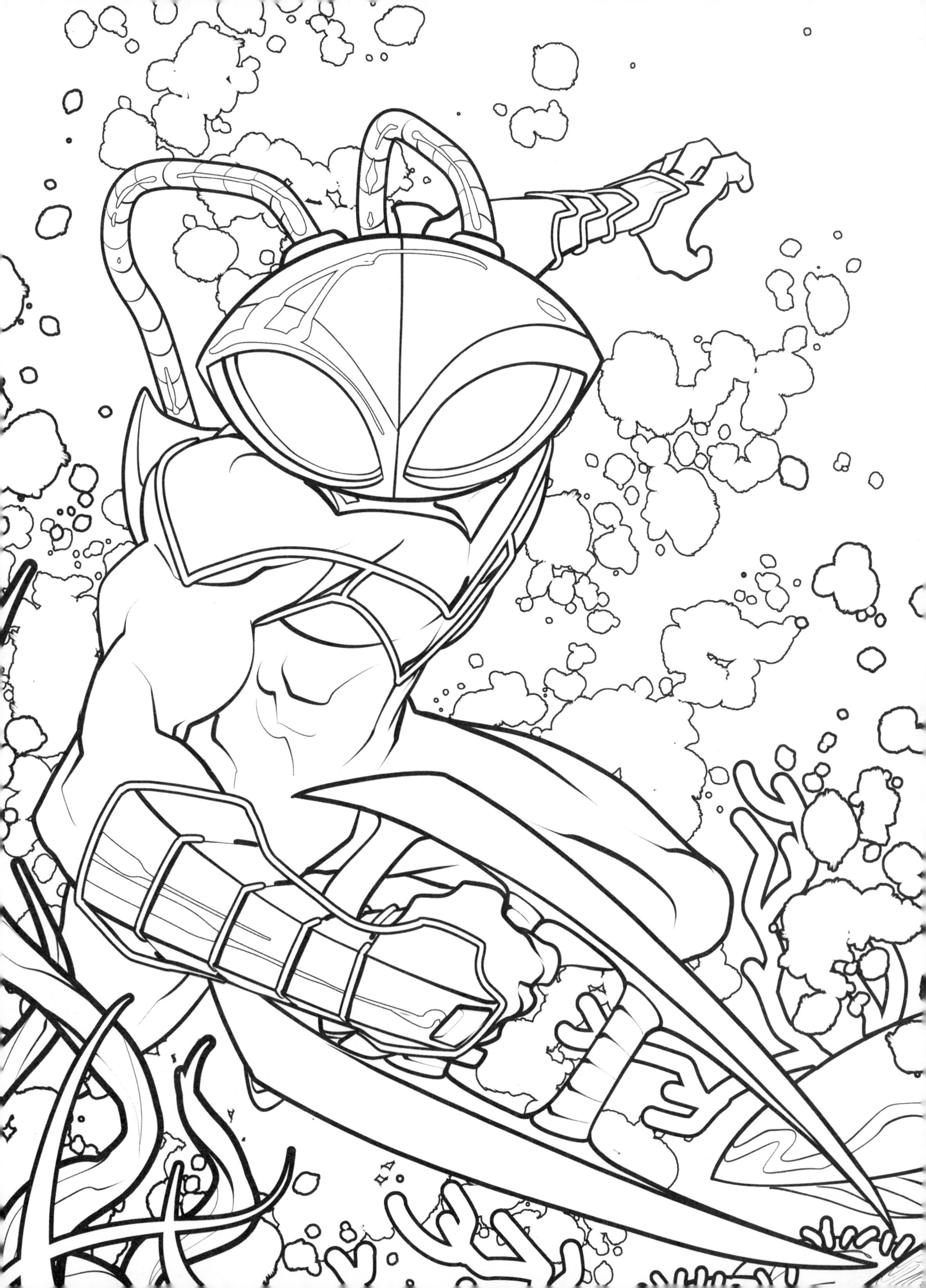

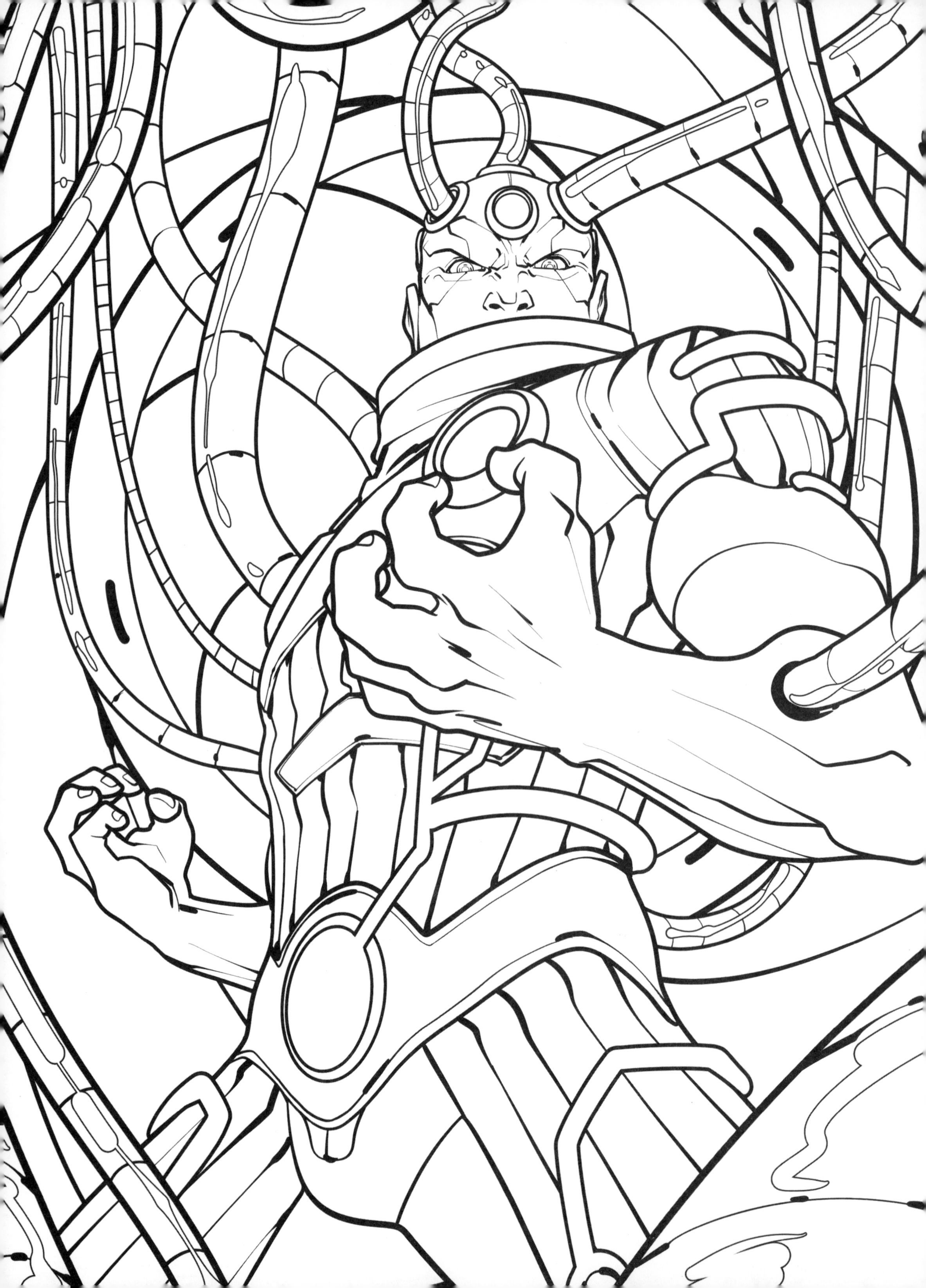

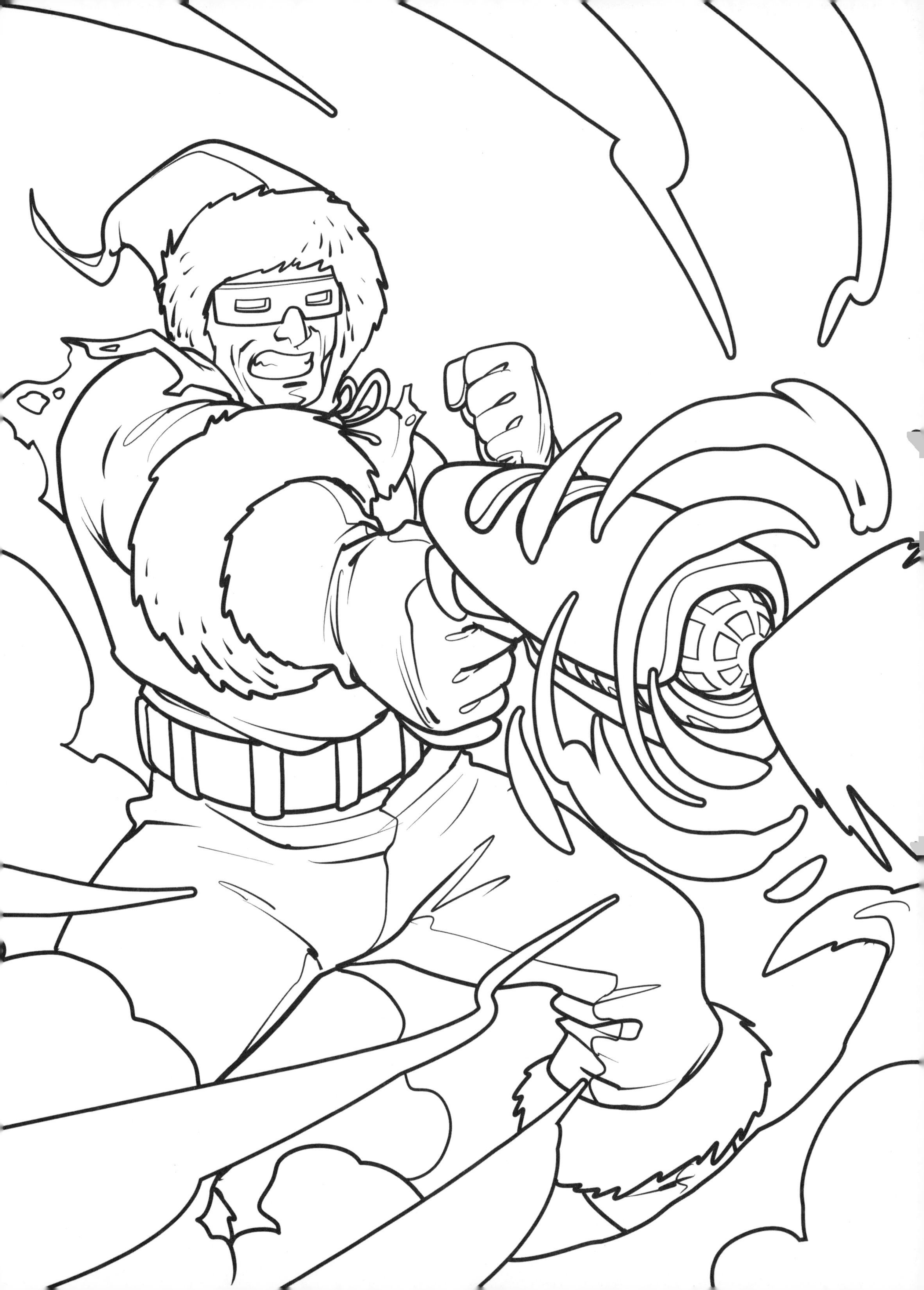

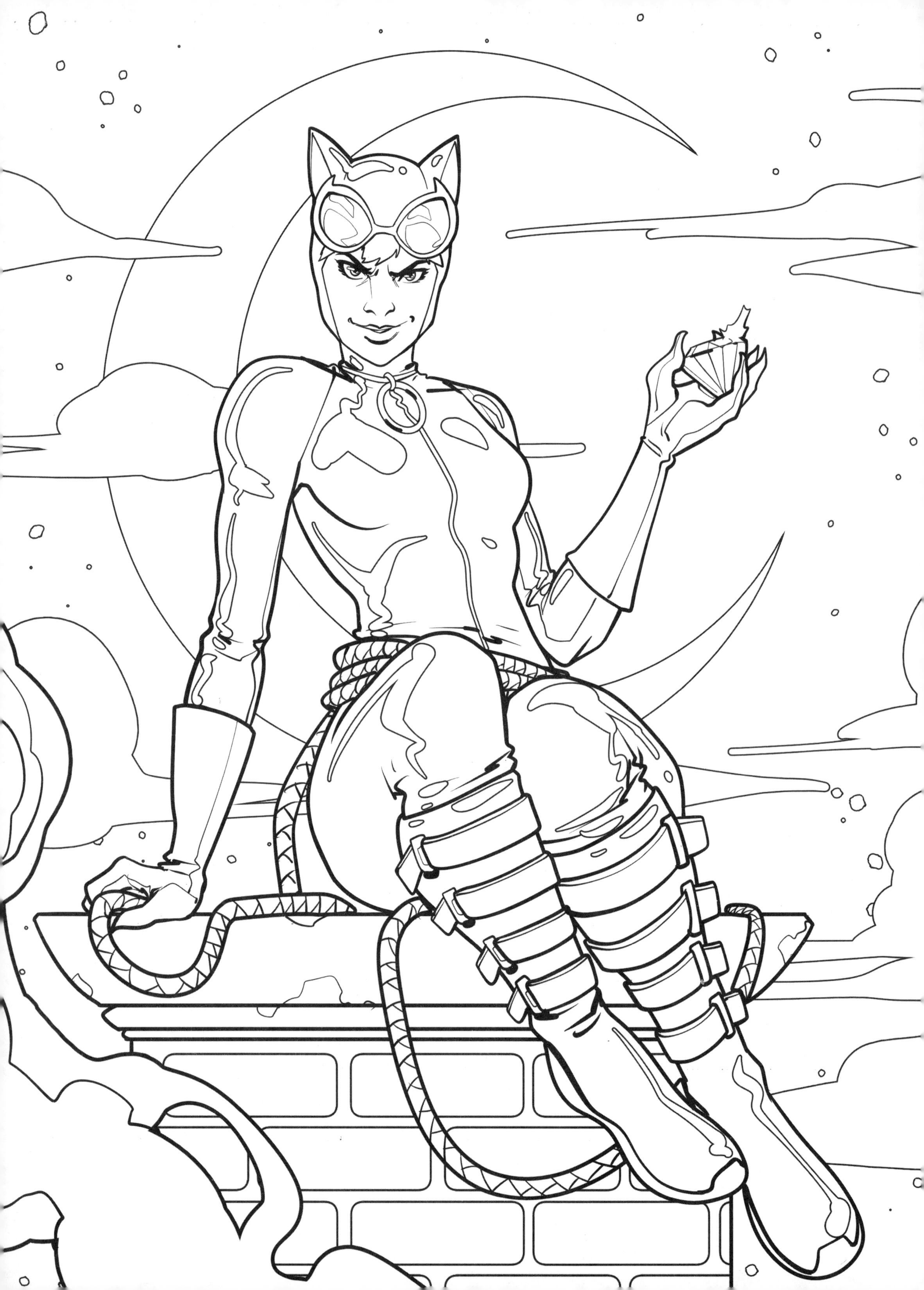

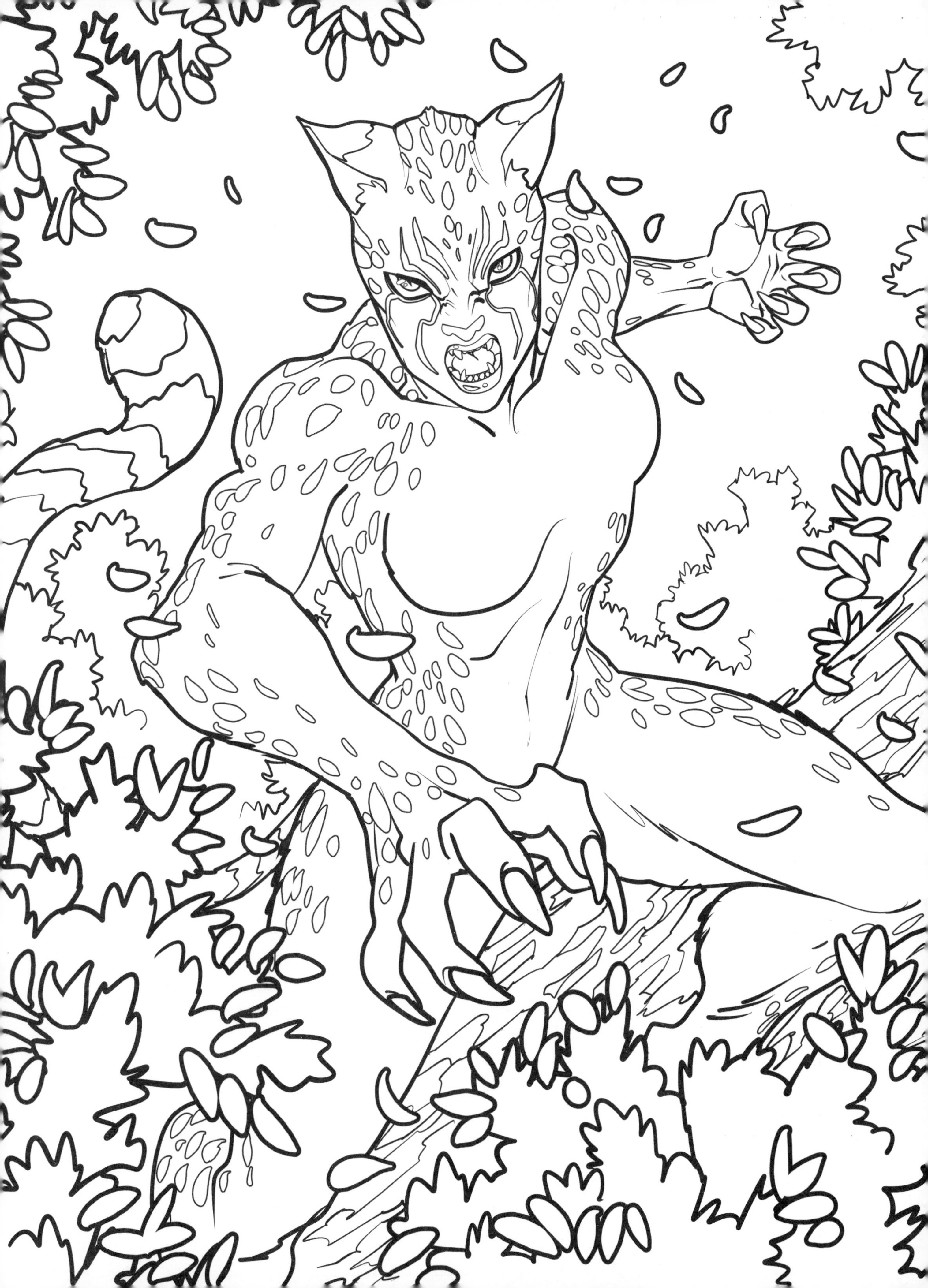

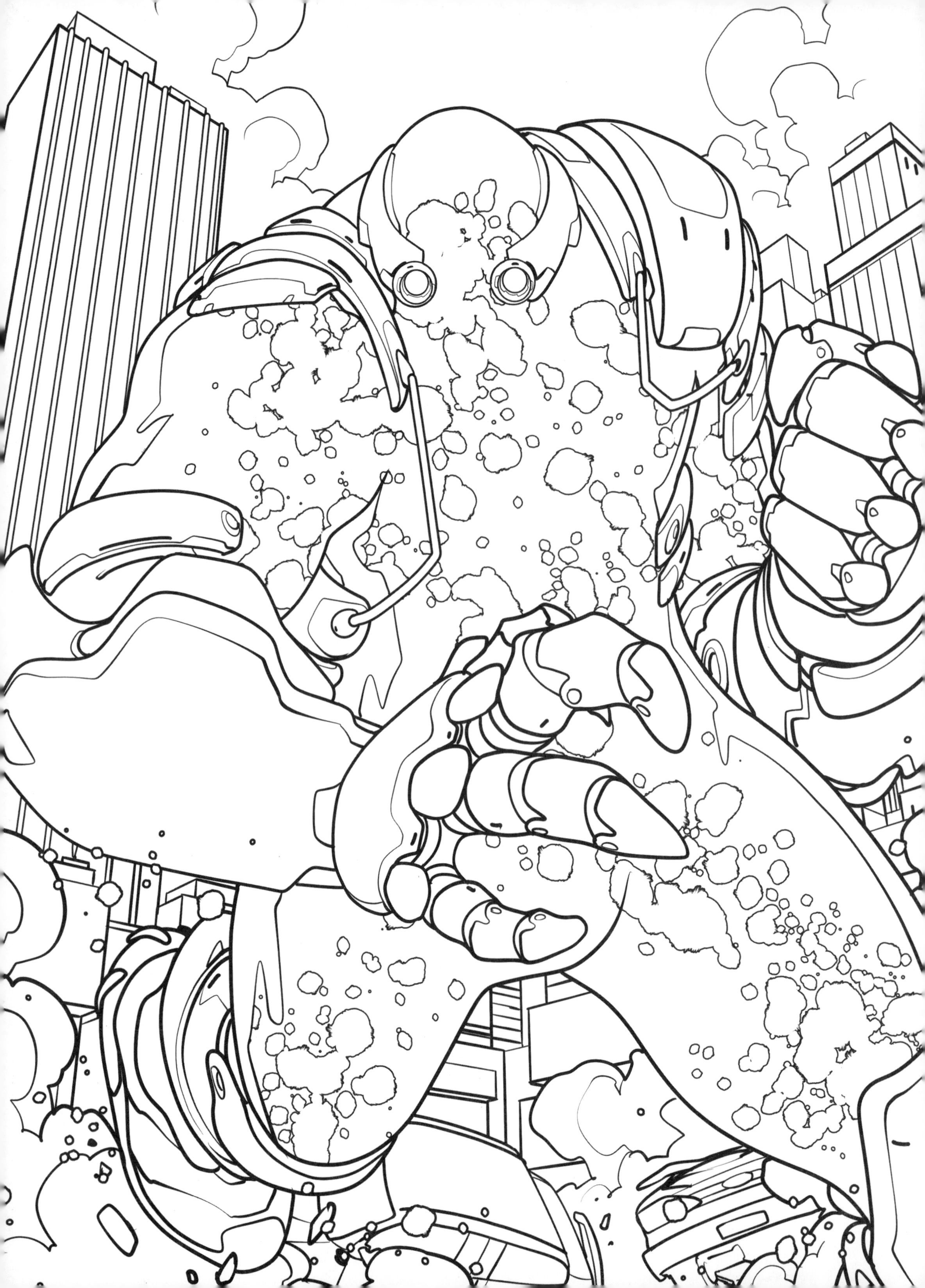

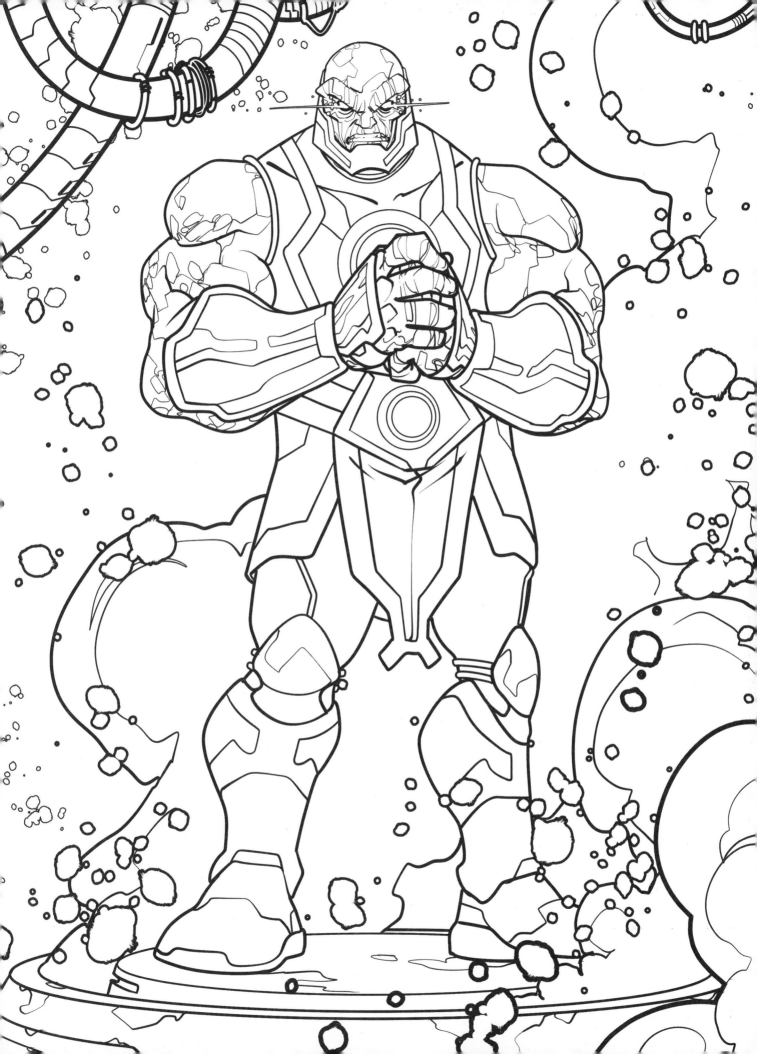

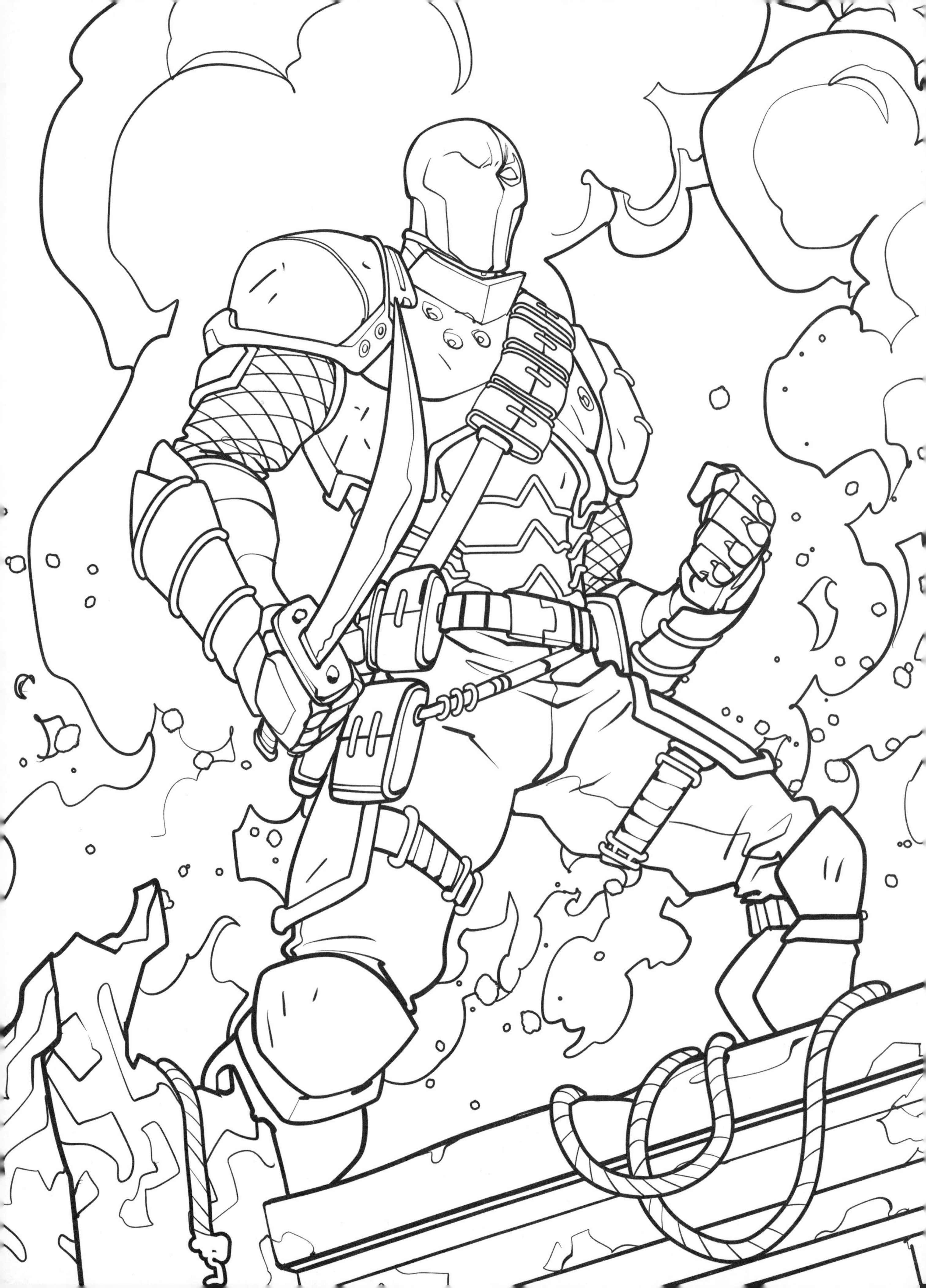

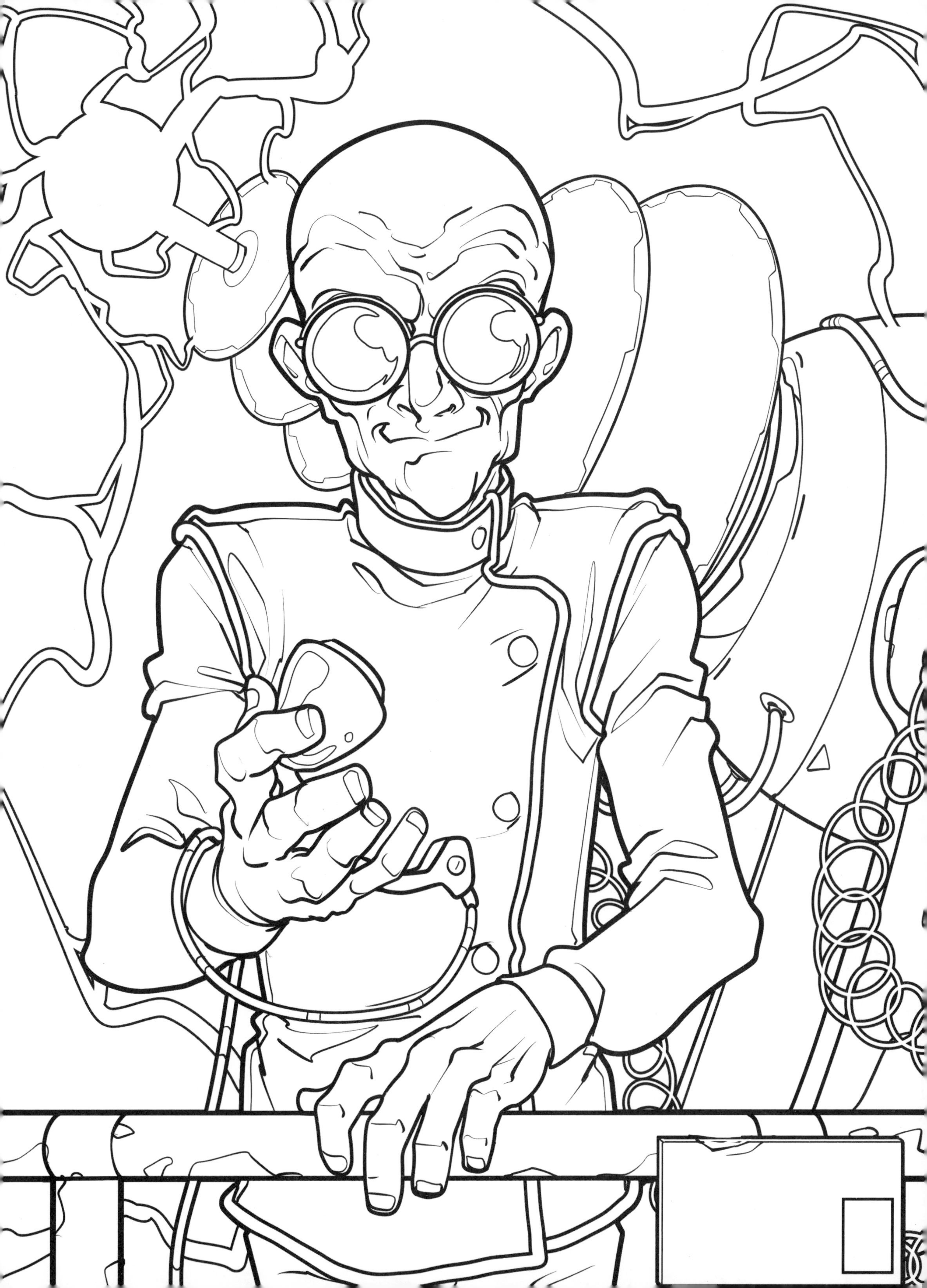

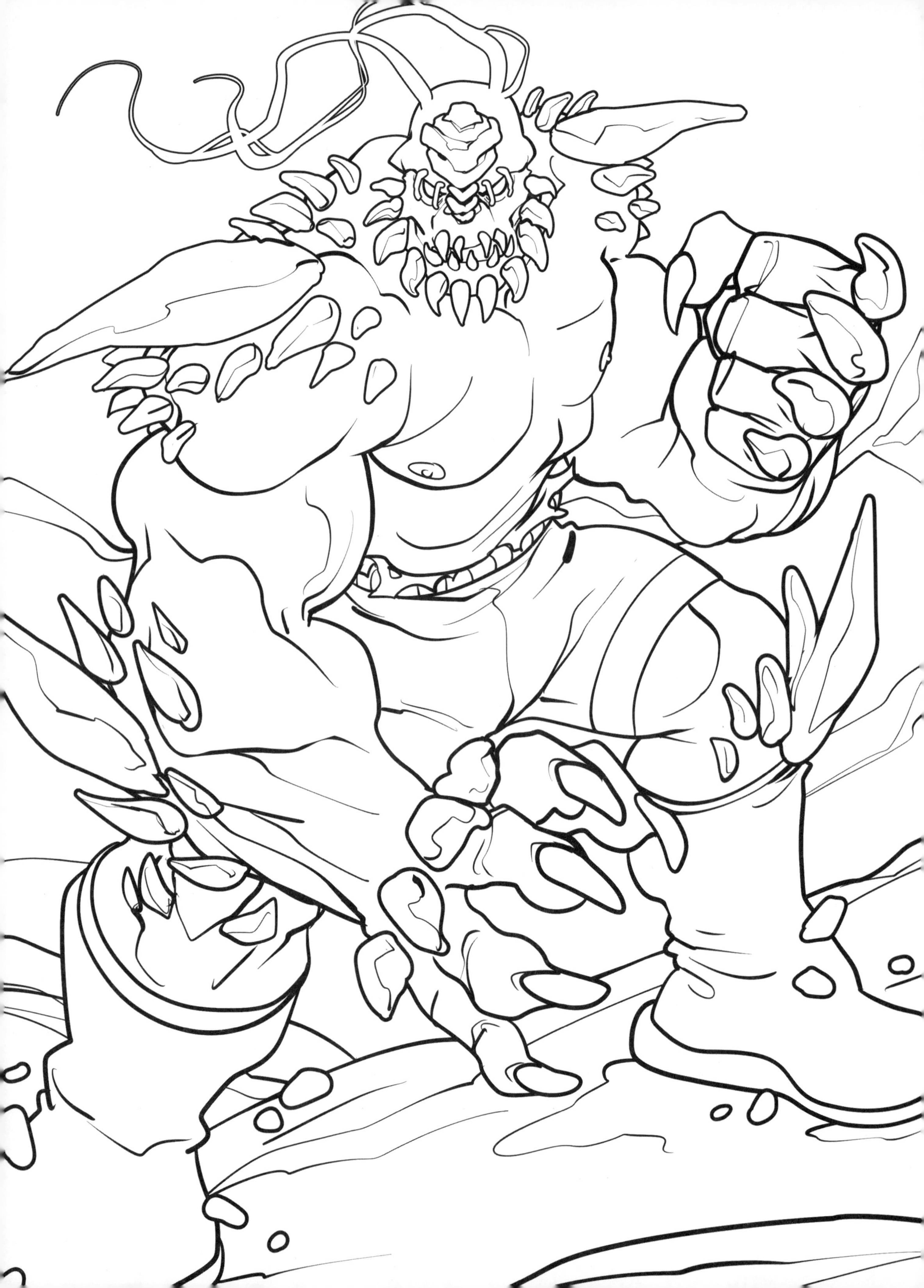

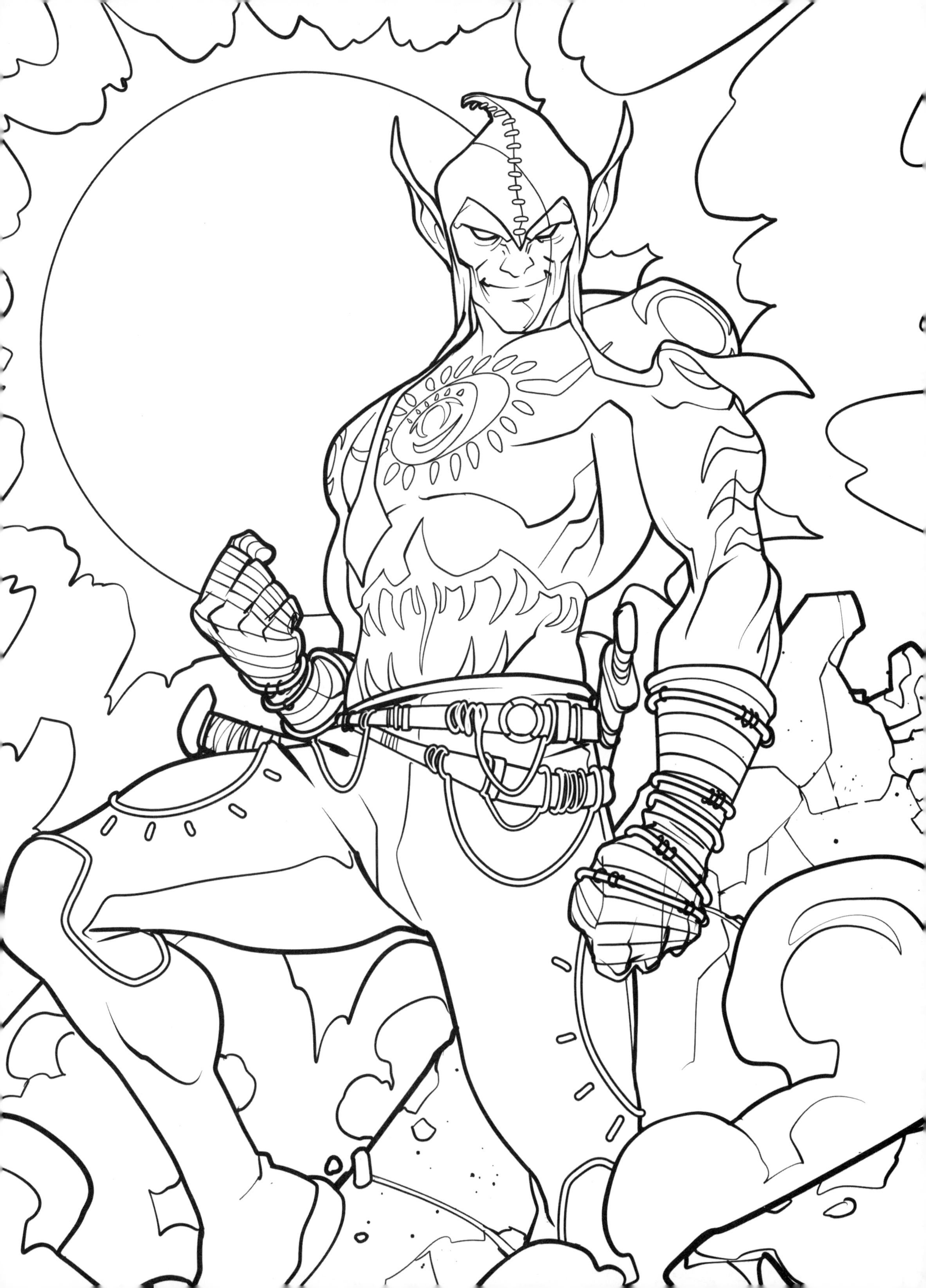

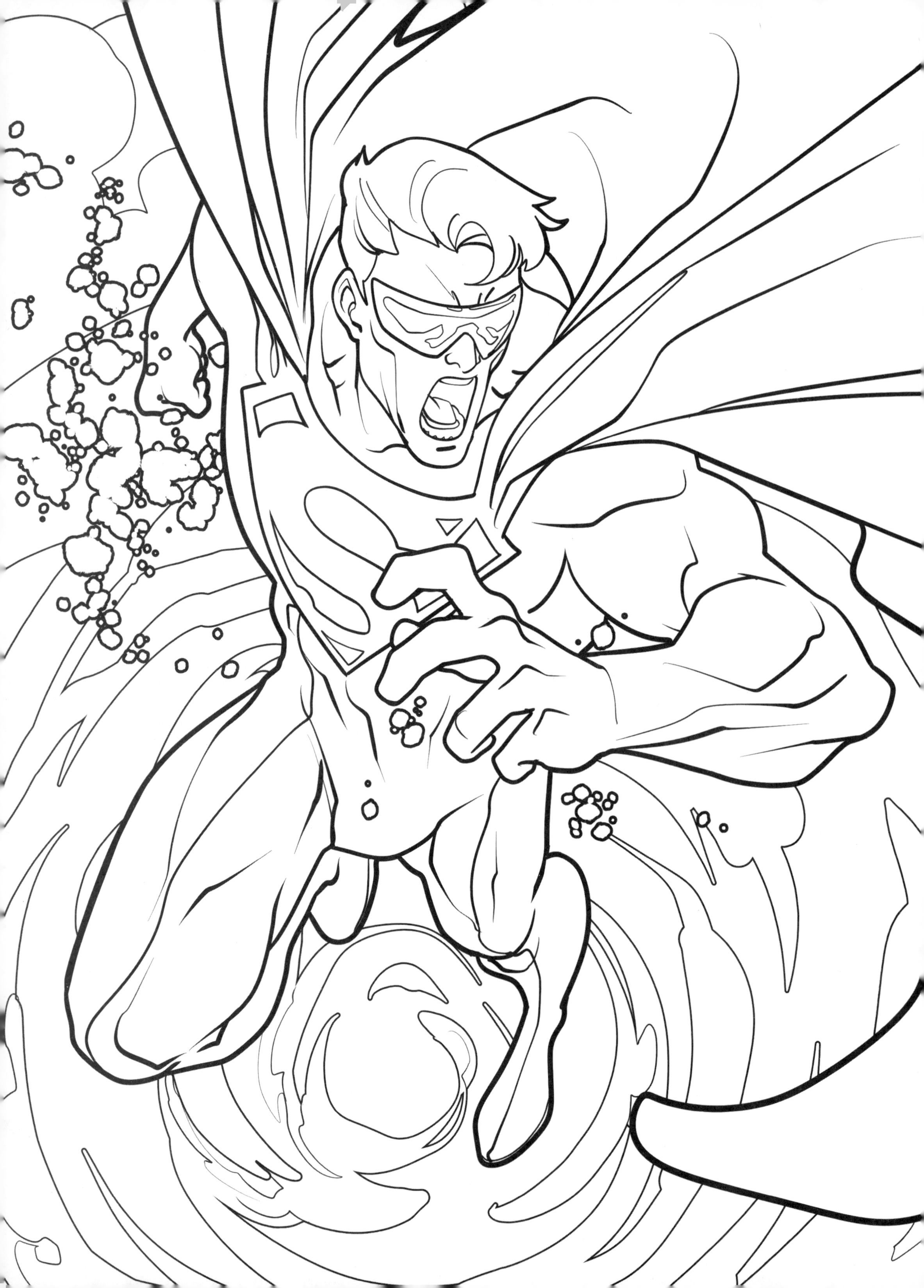

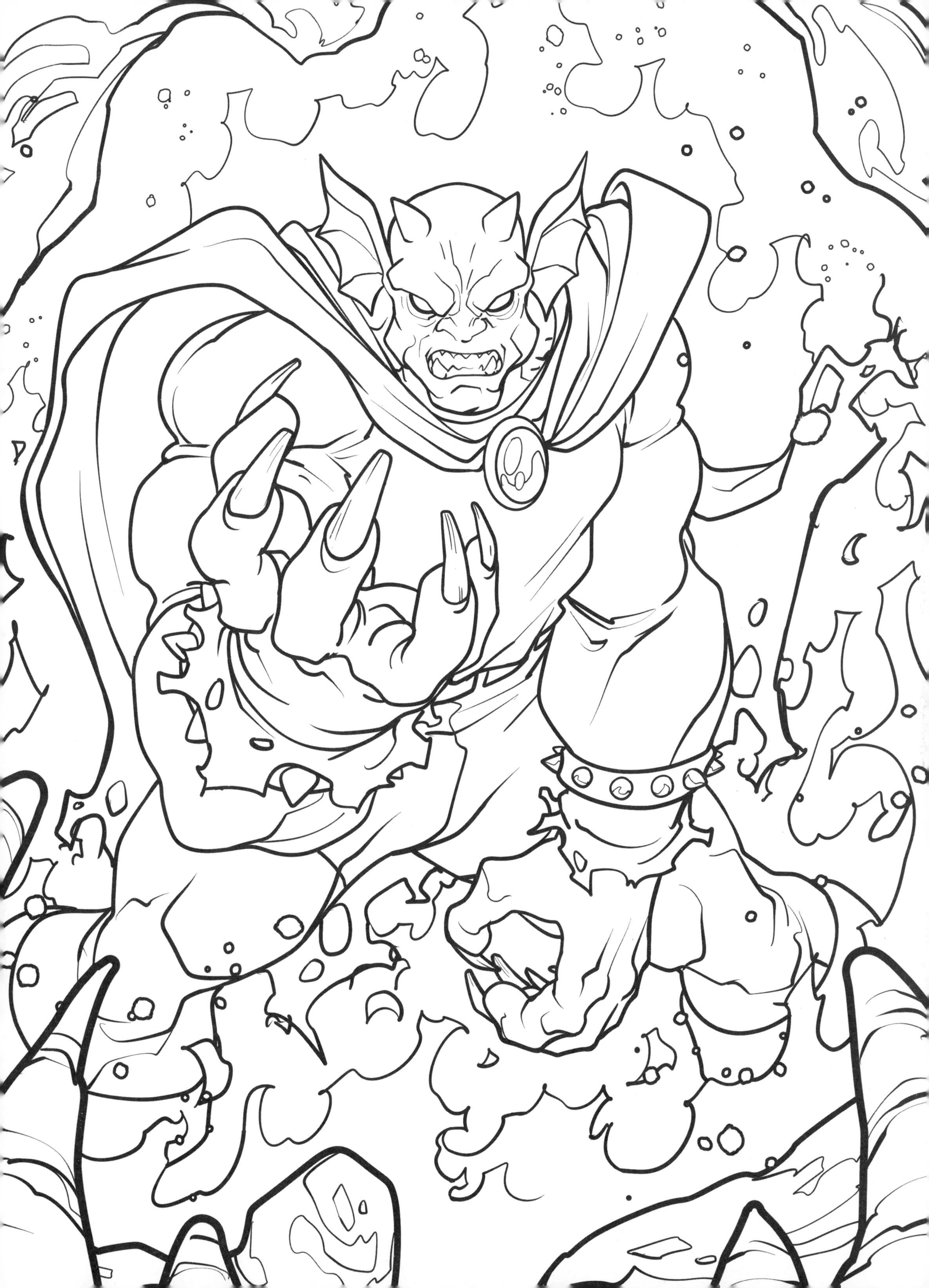

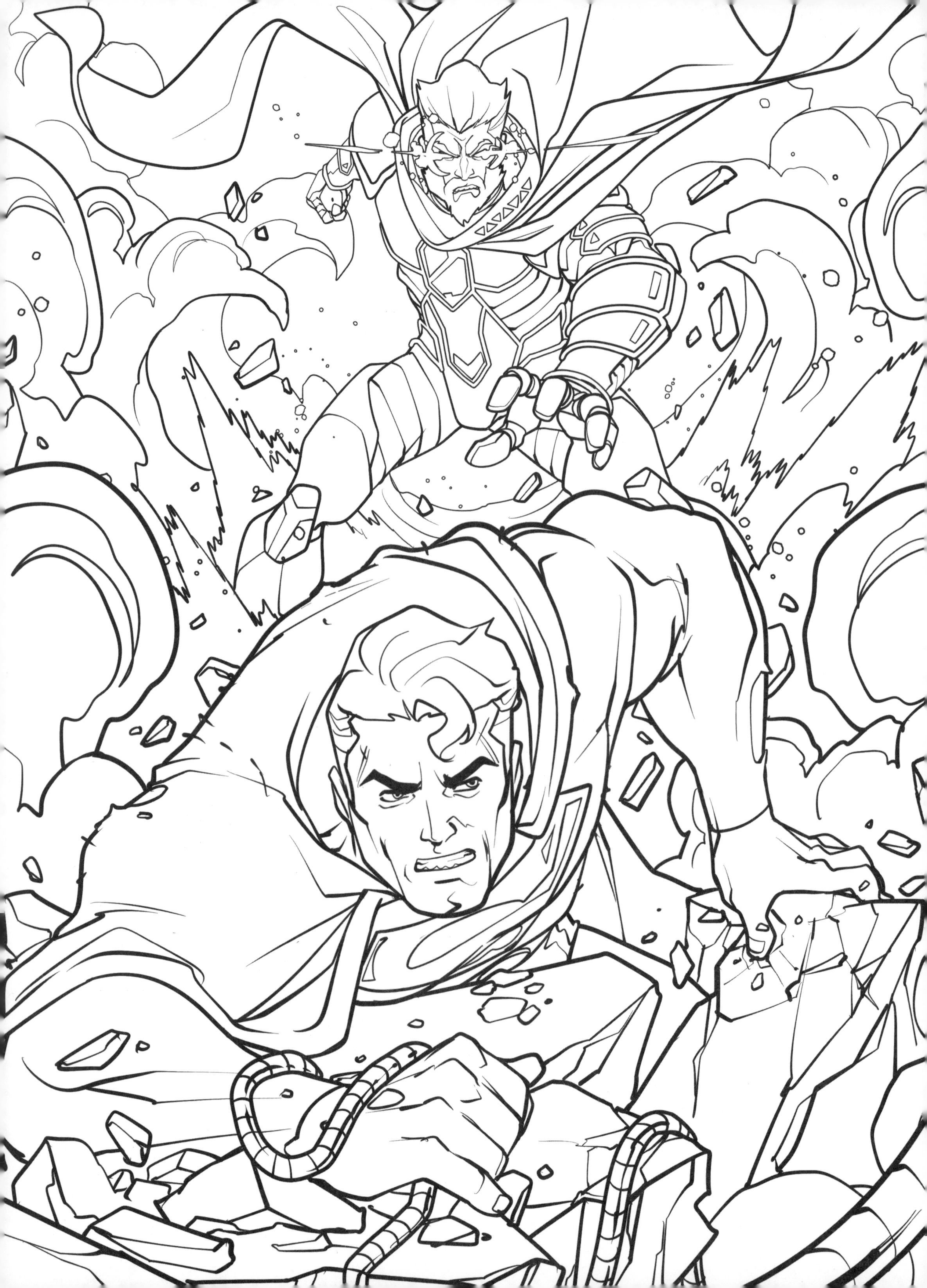

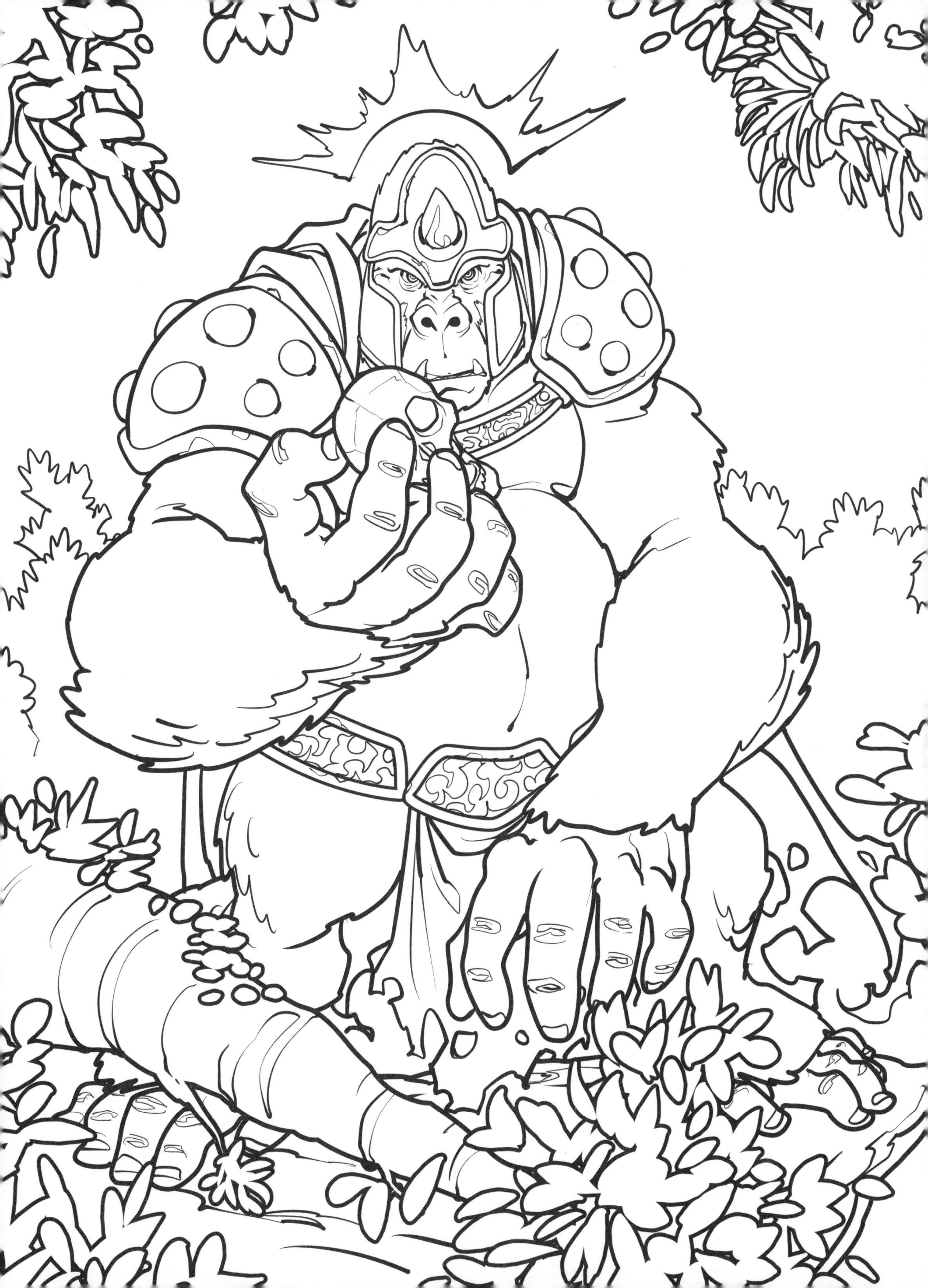

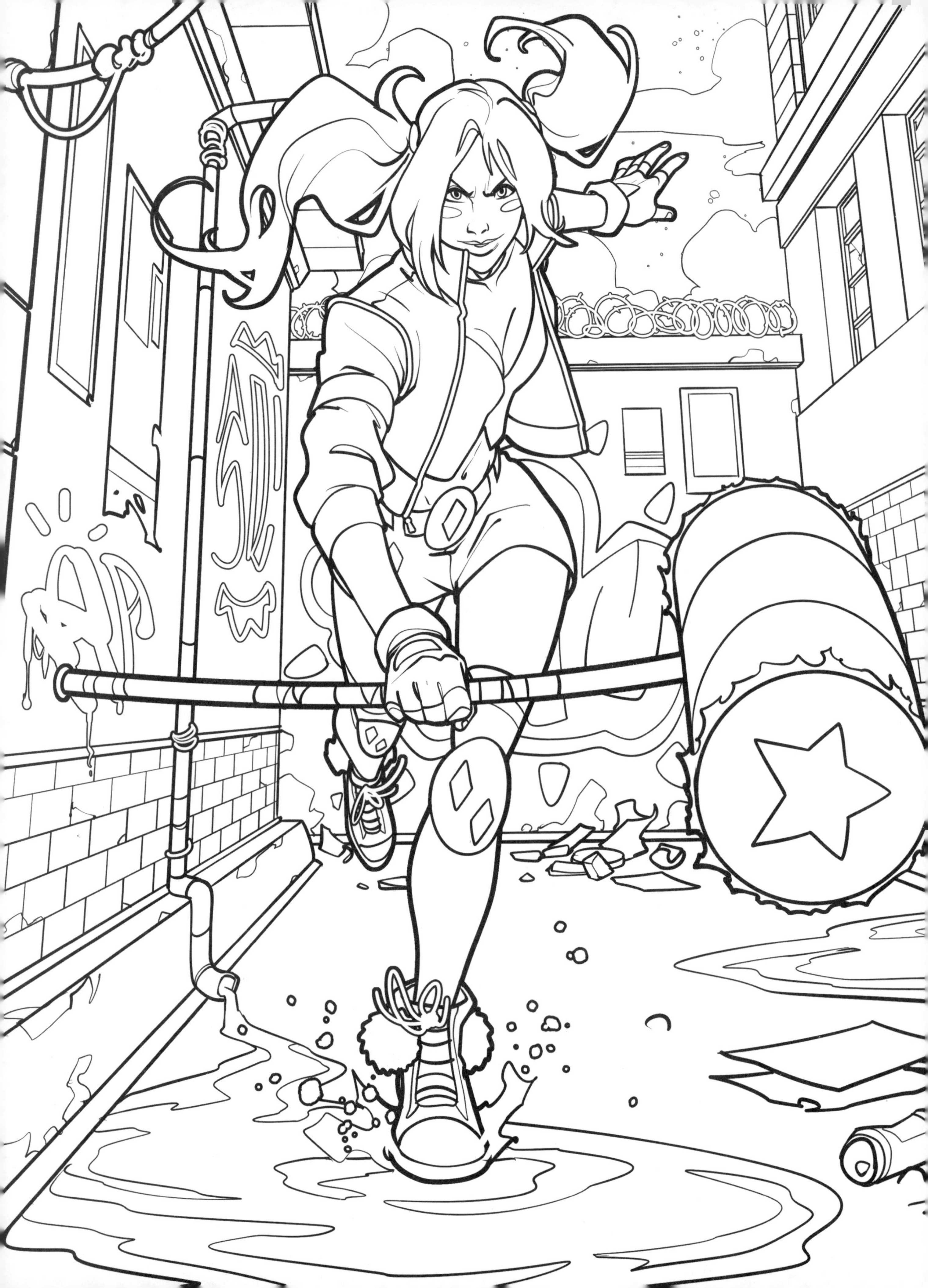

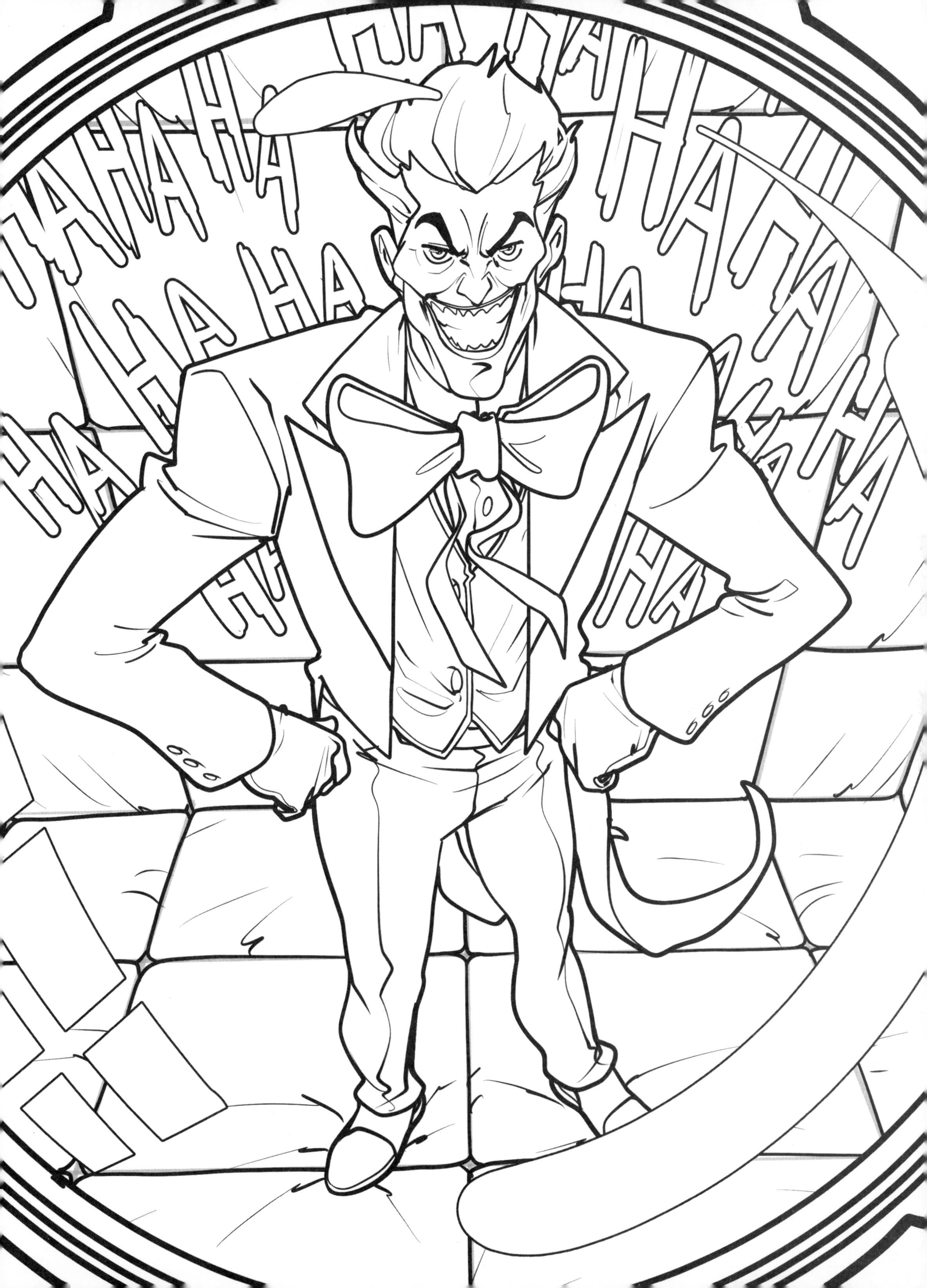
HAHAHA HA
HA HA HA
HA HA
HA
HA HA HA HA

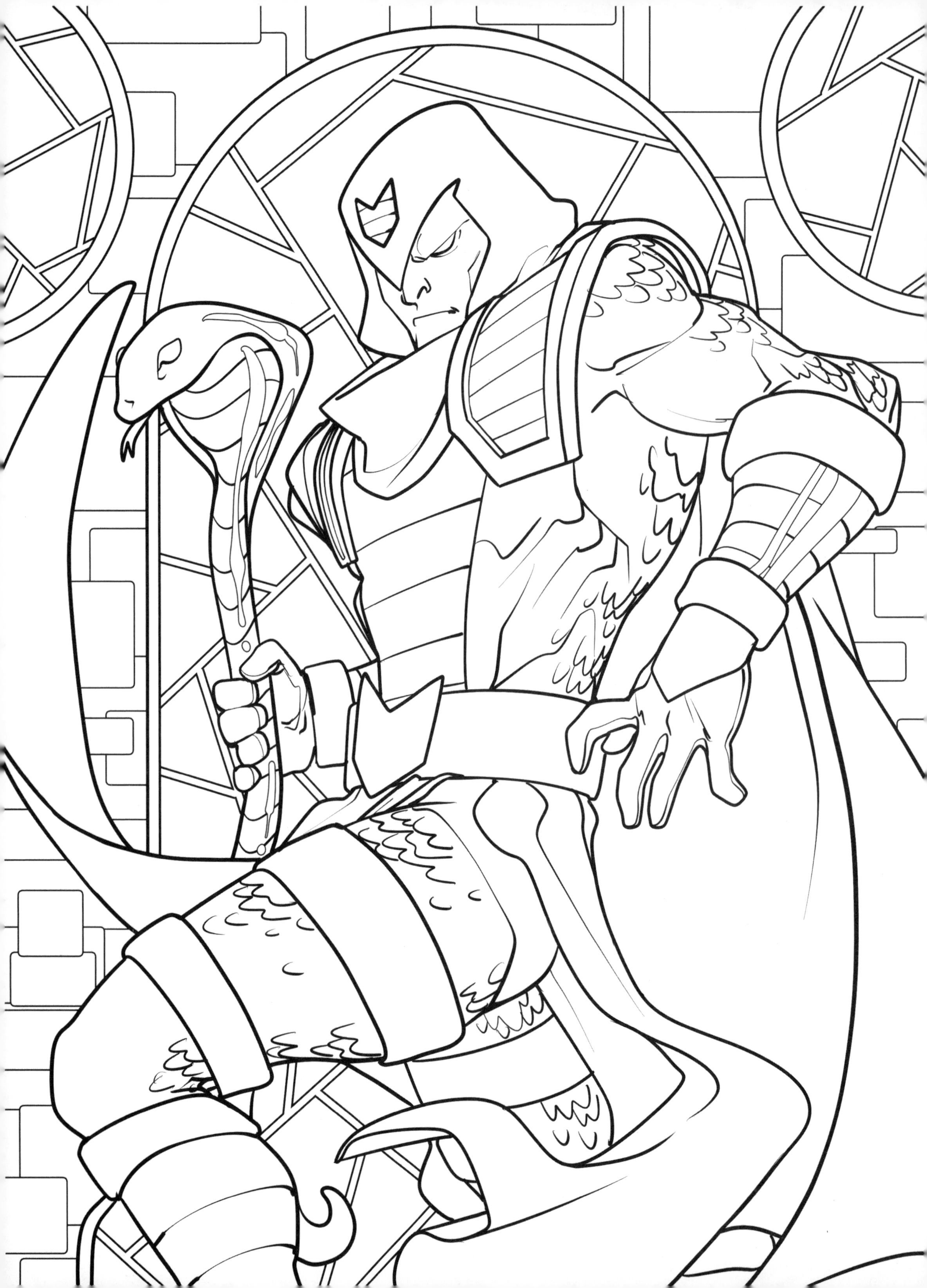

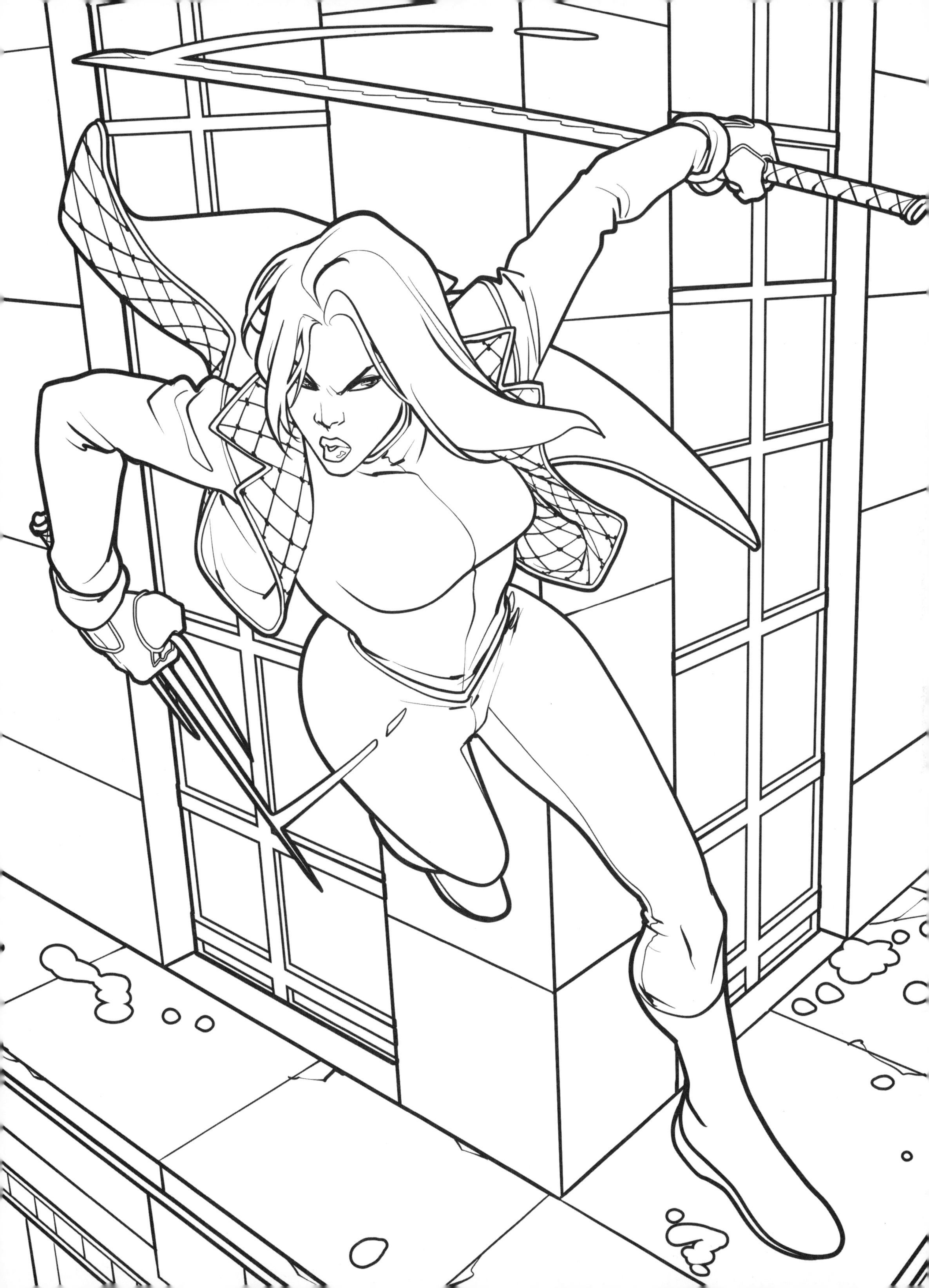

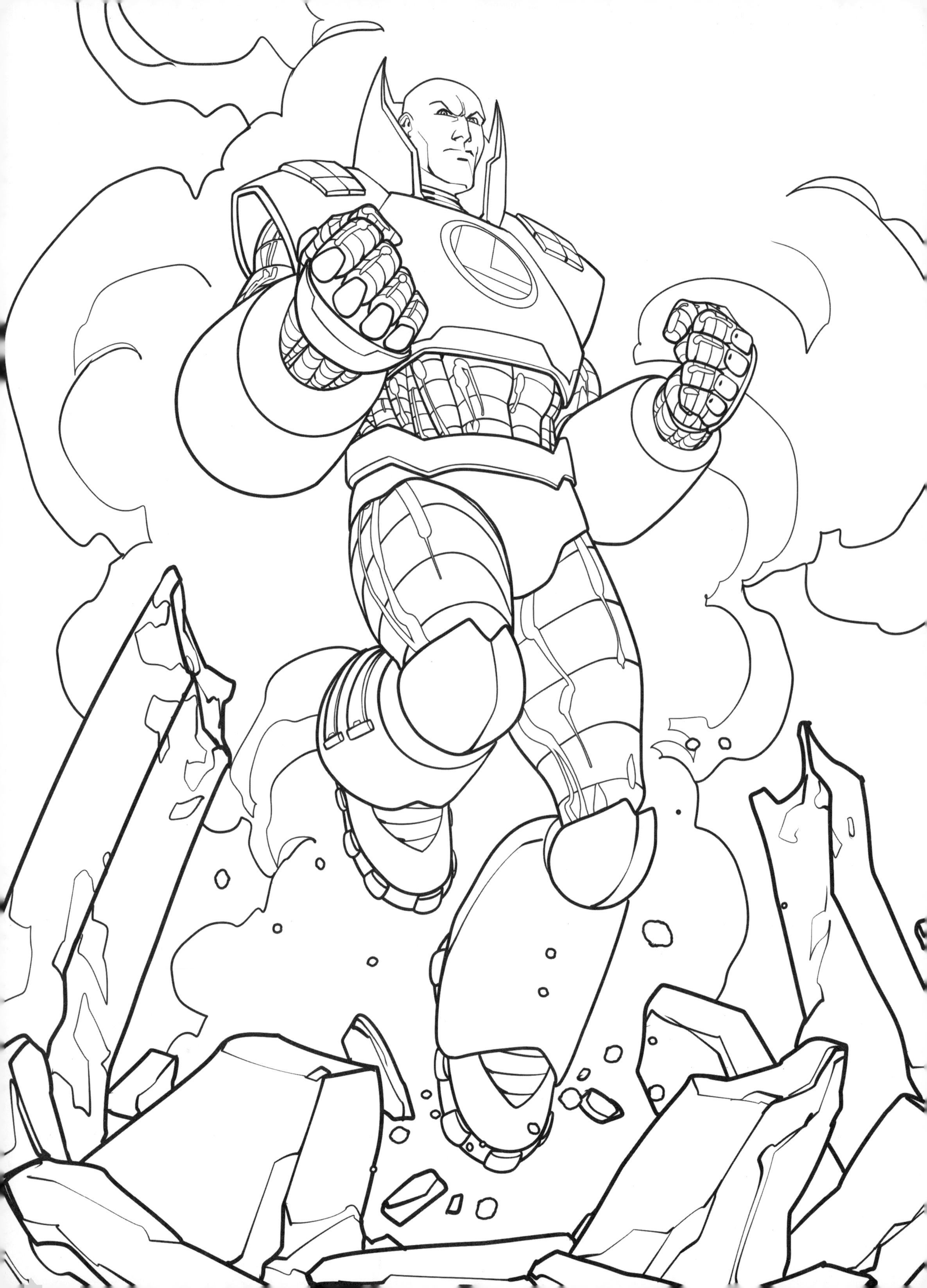

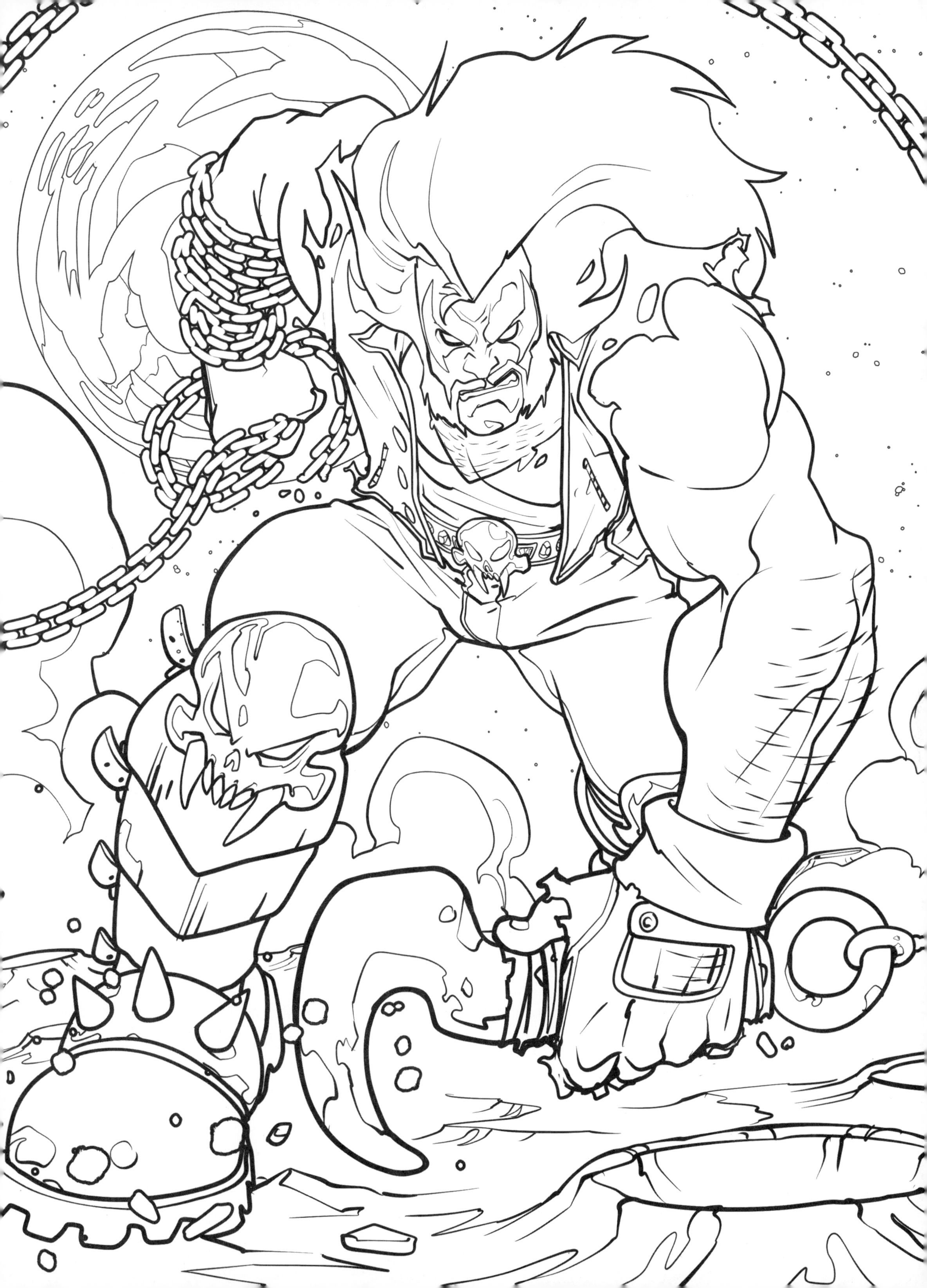

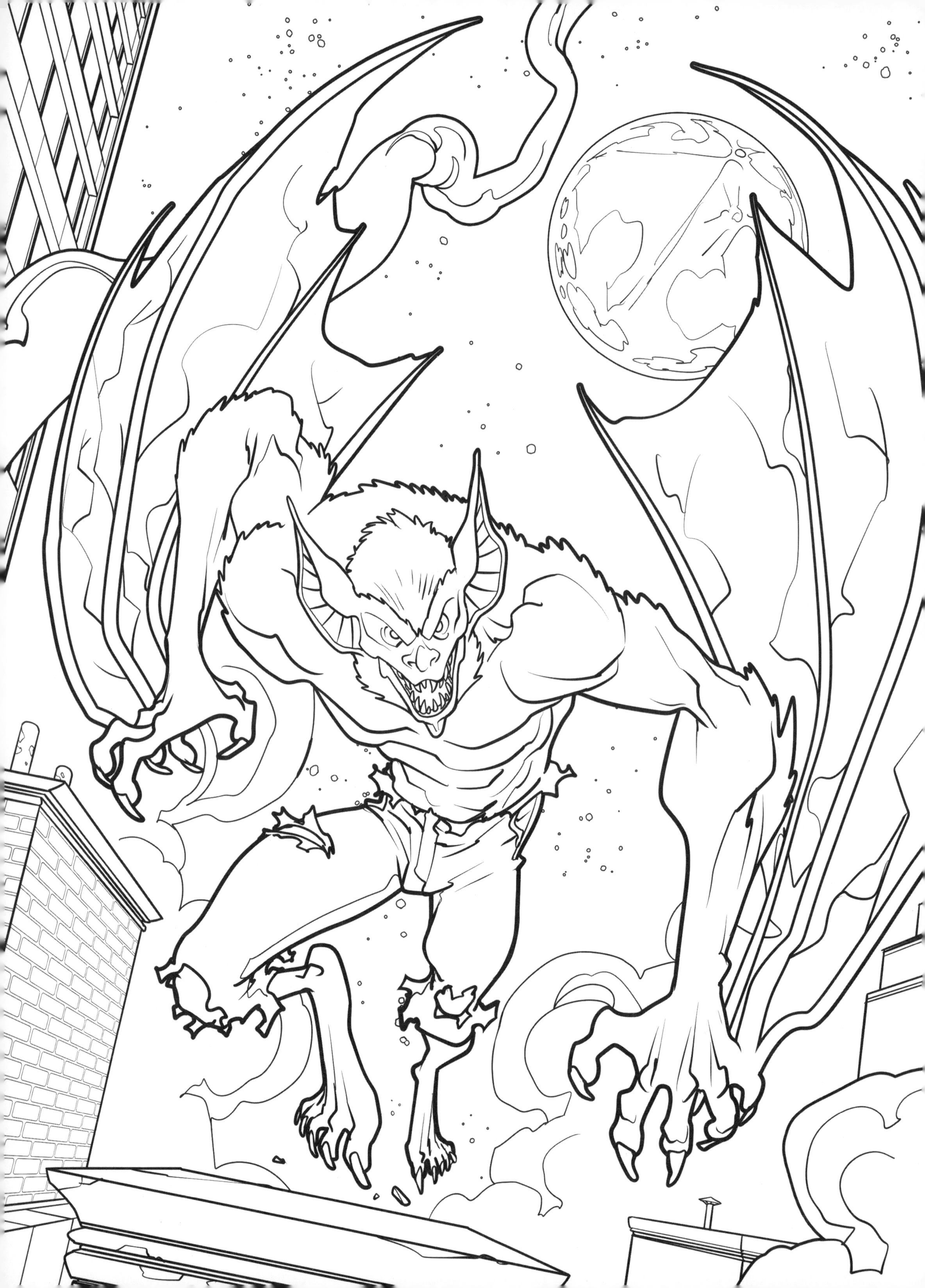

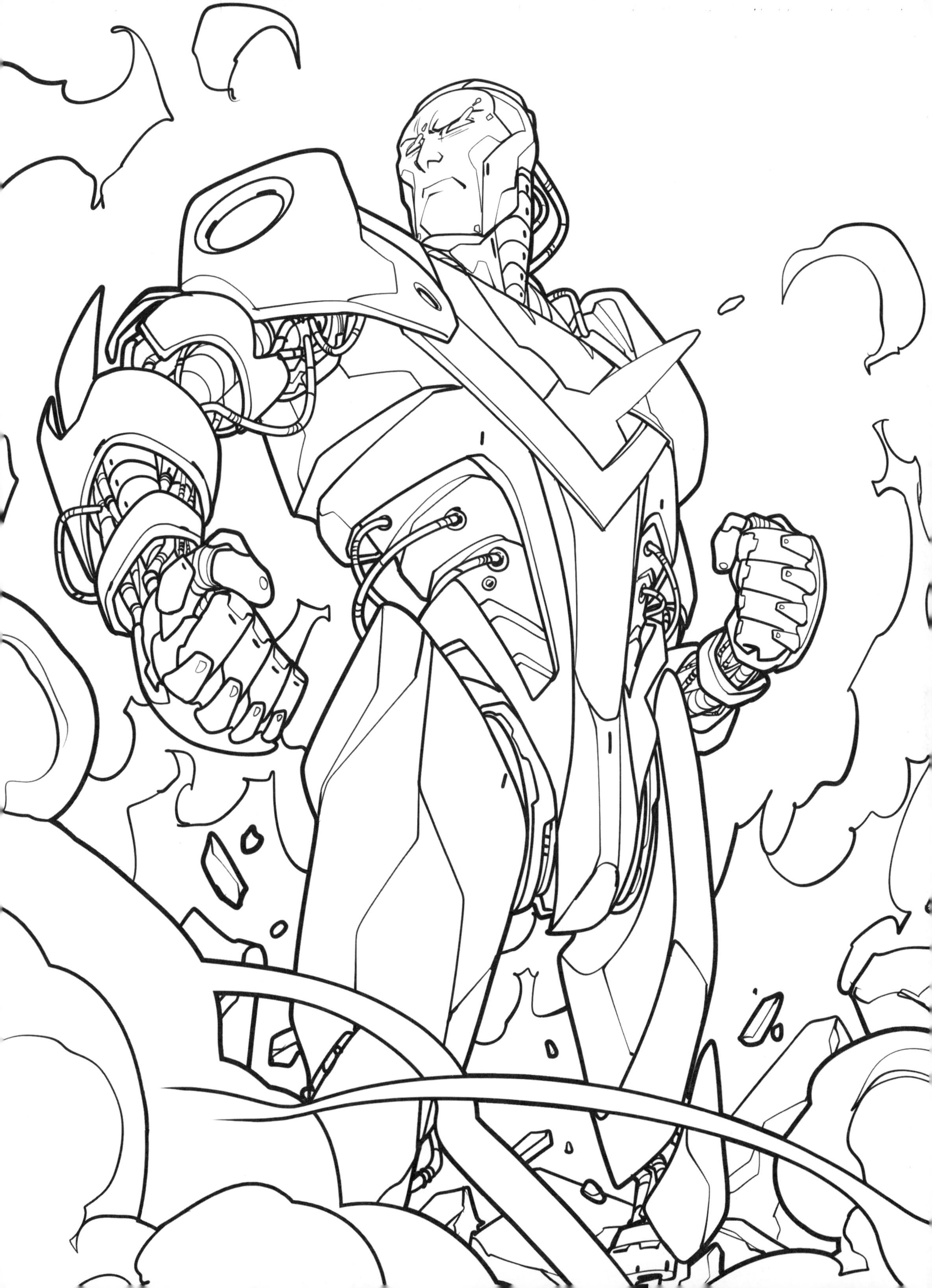

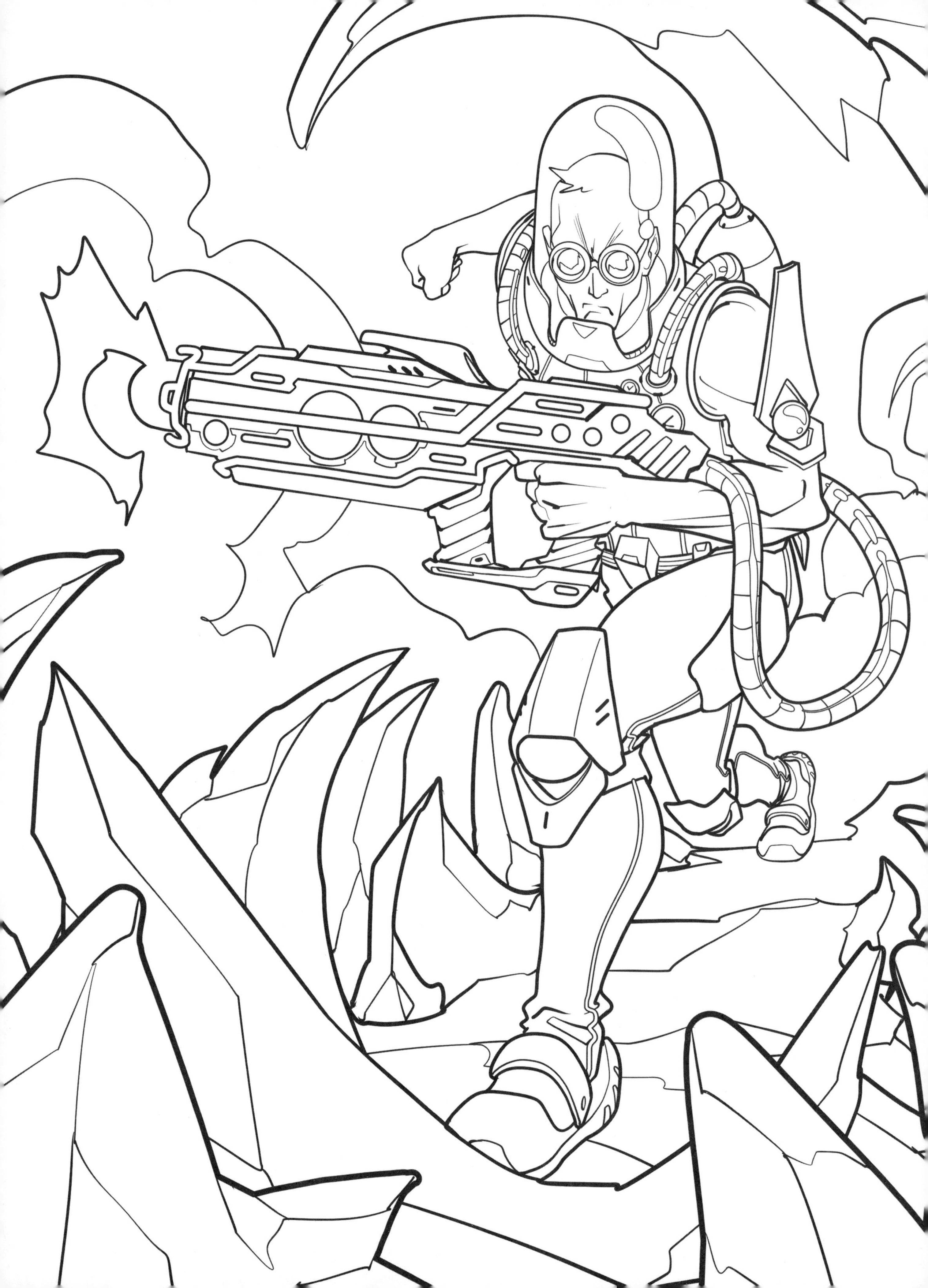

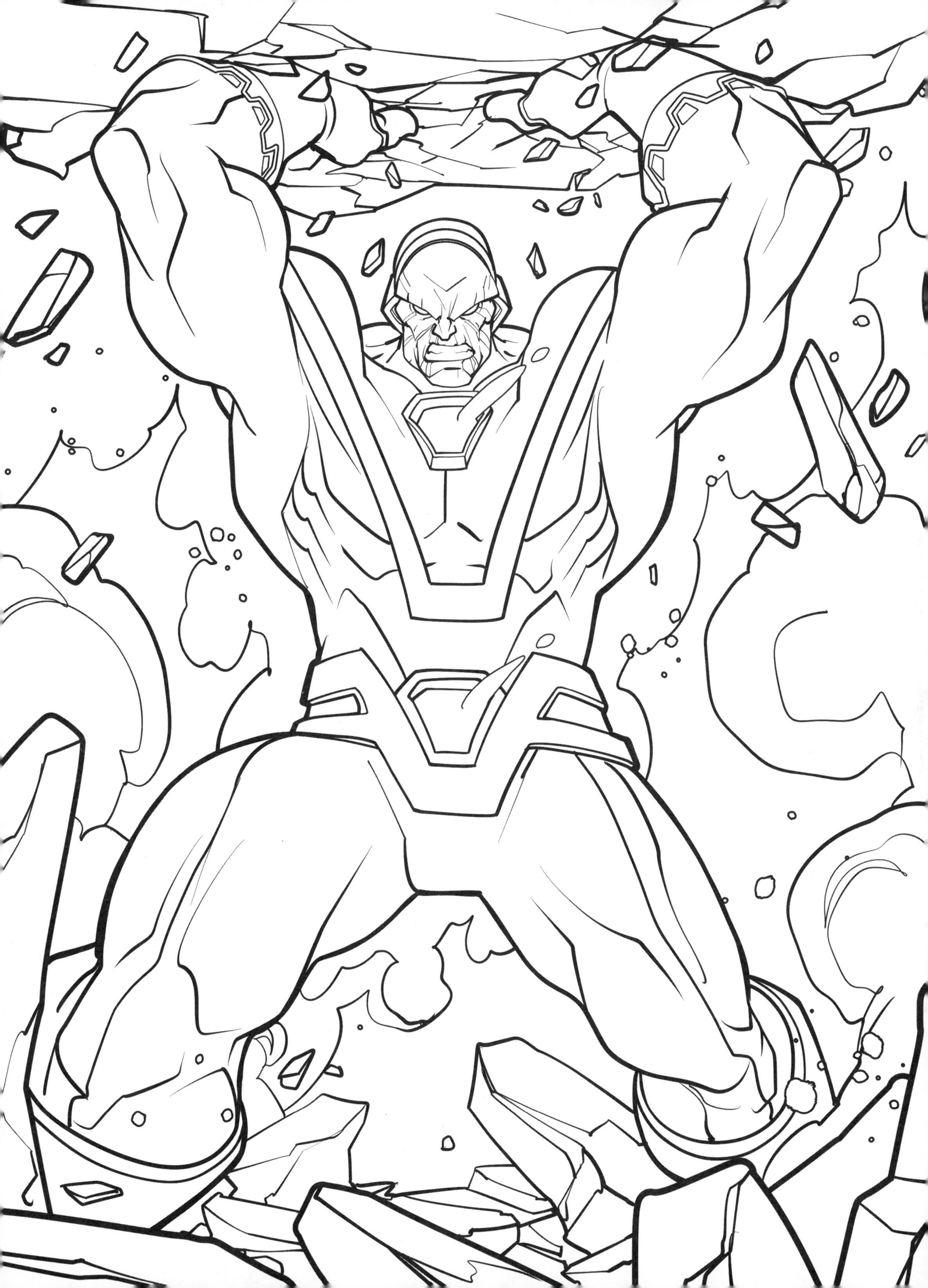

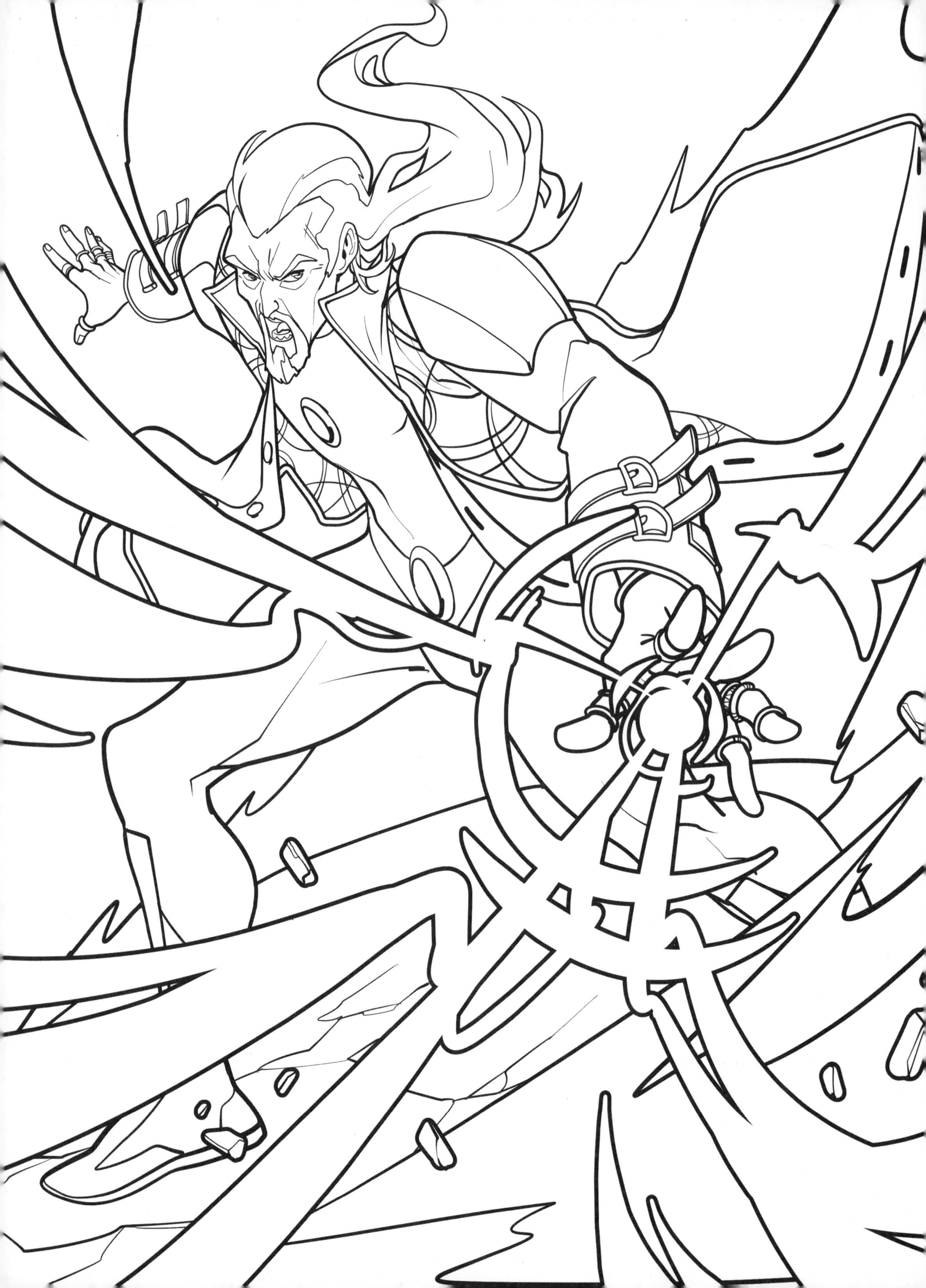

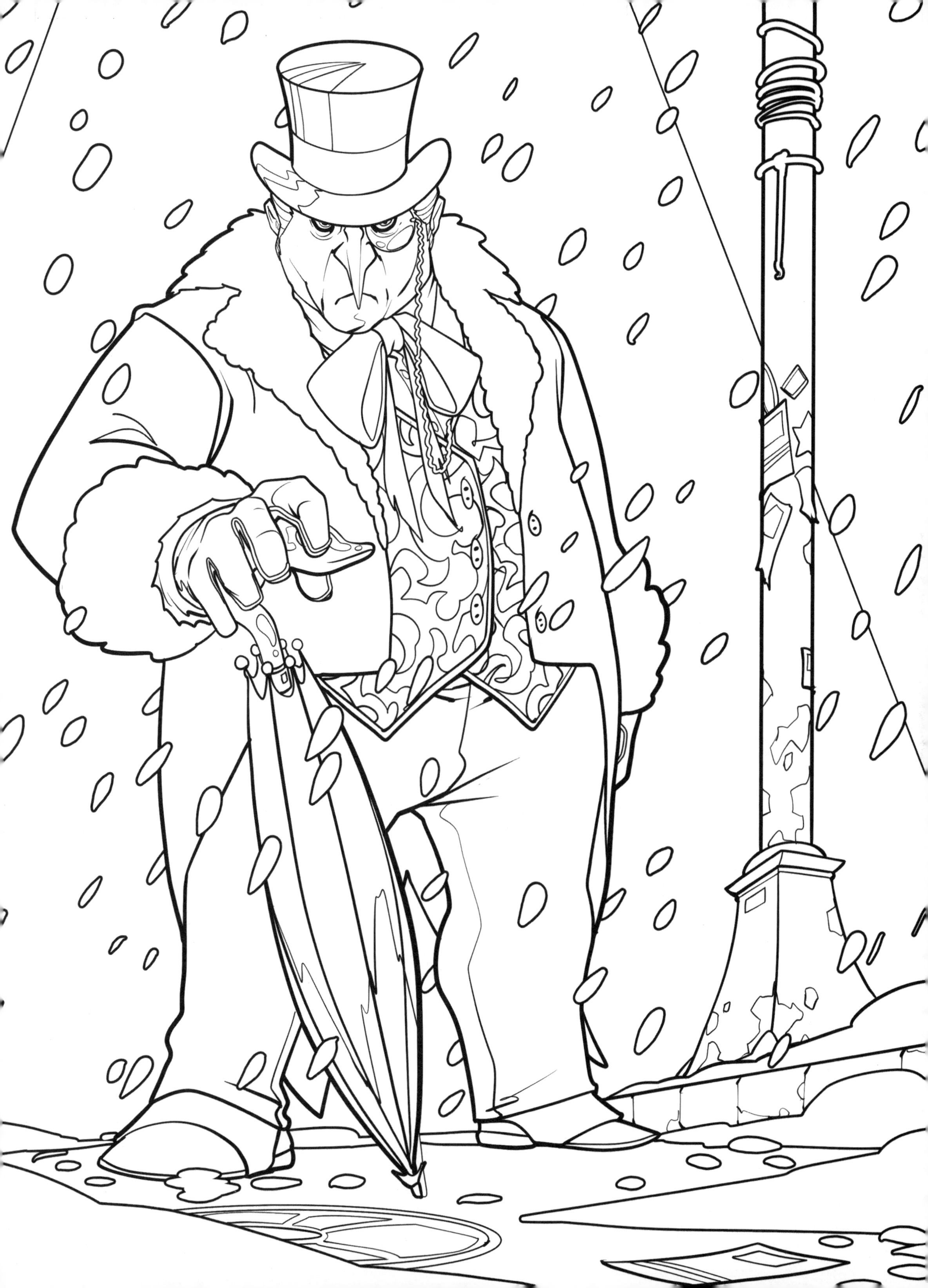

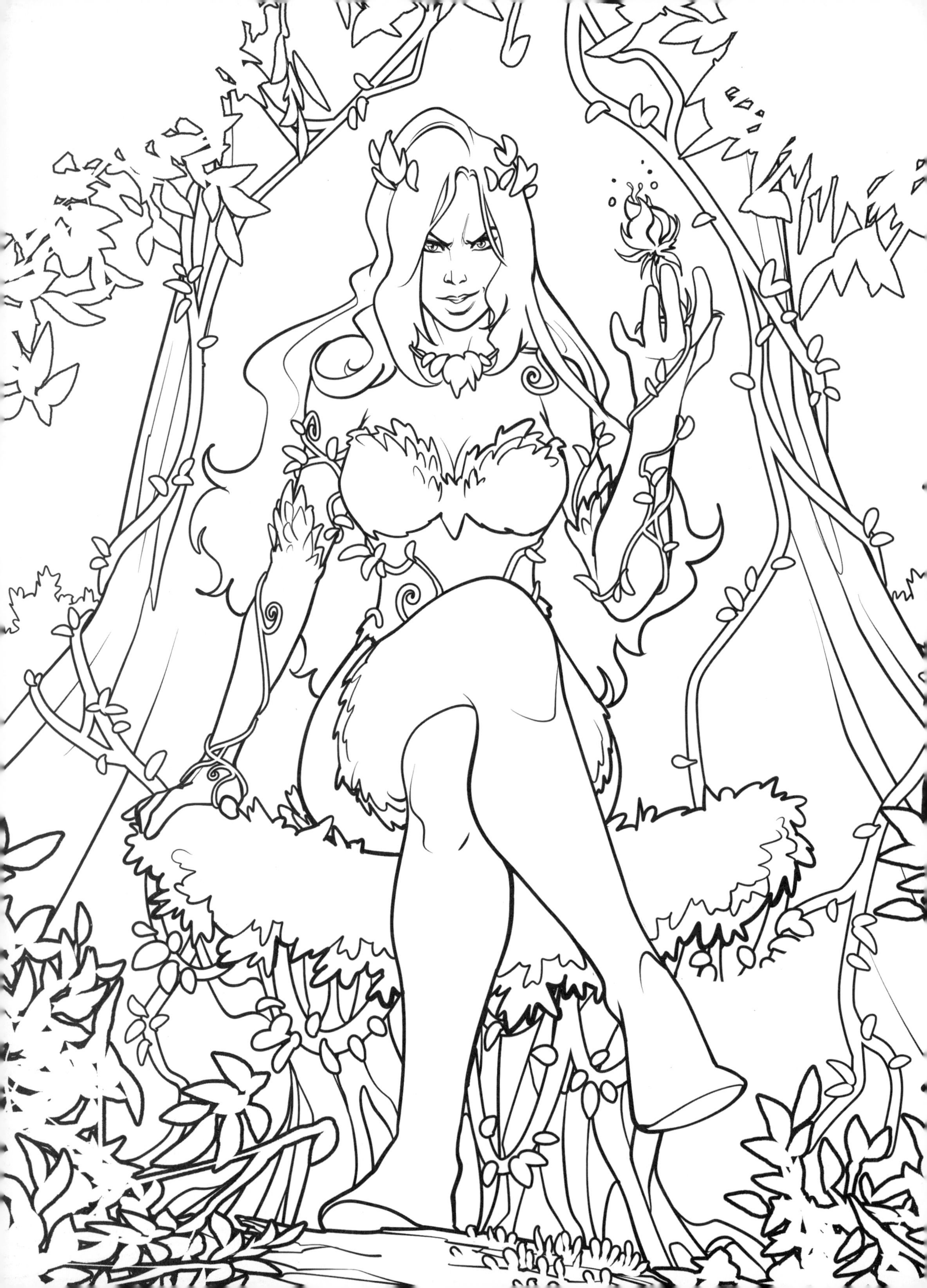

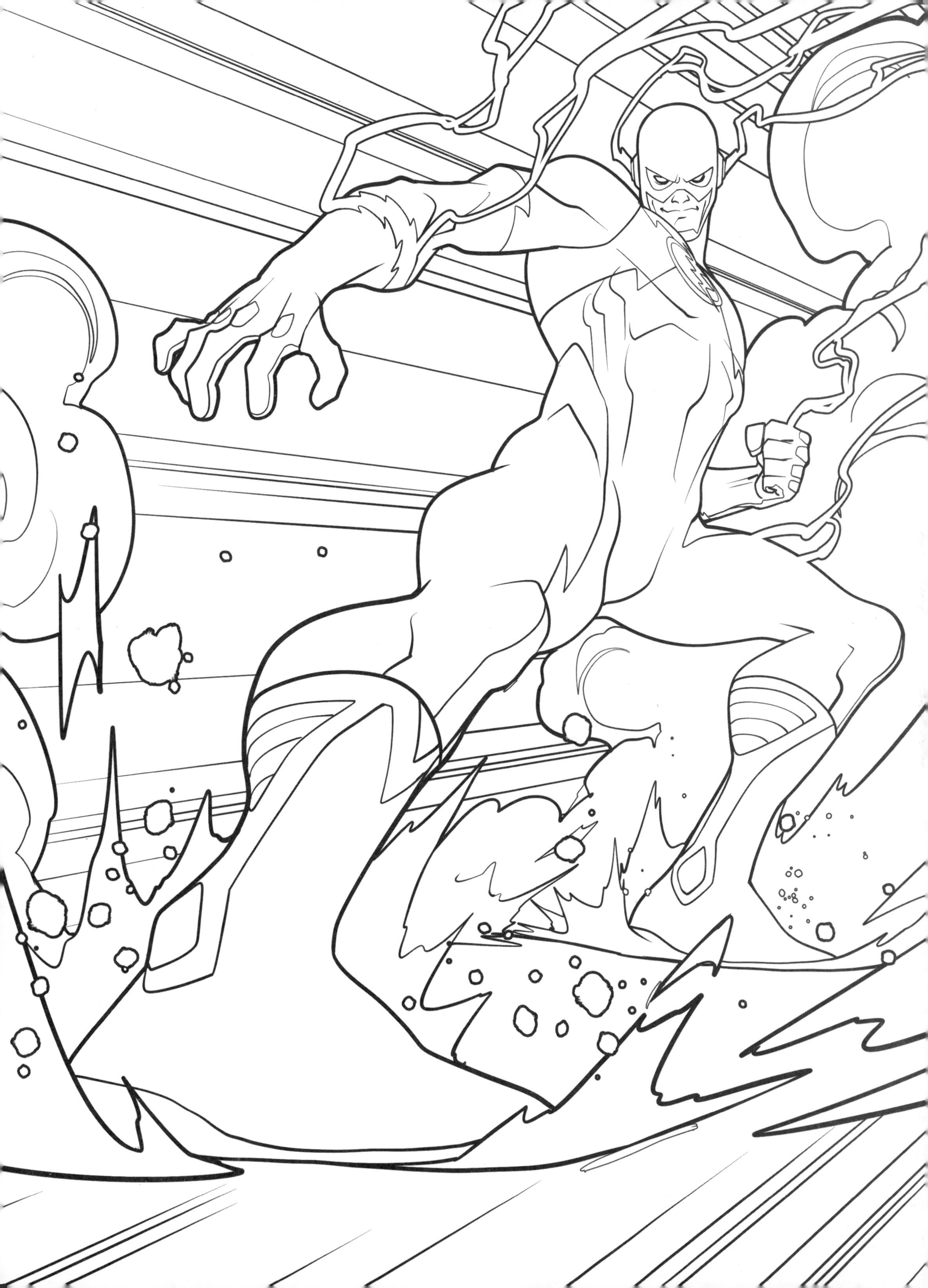

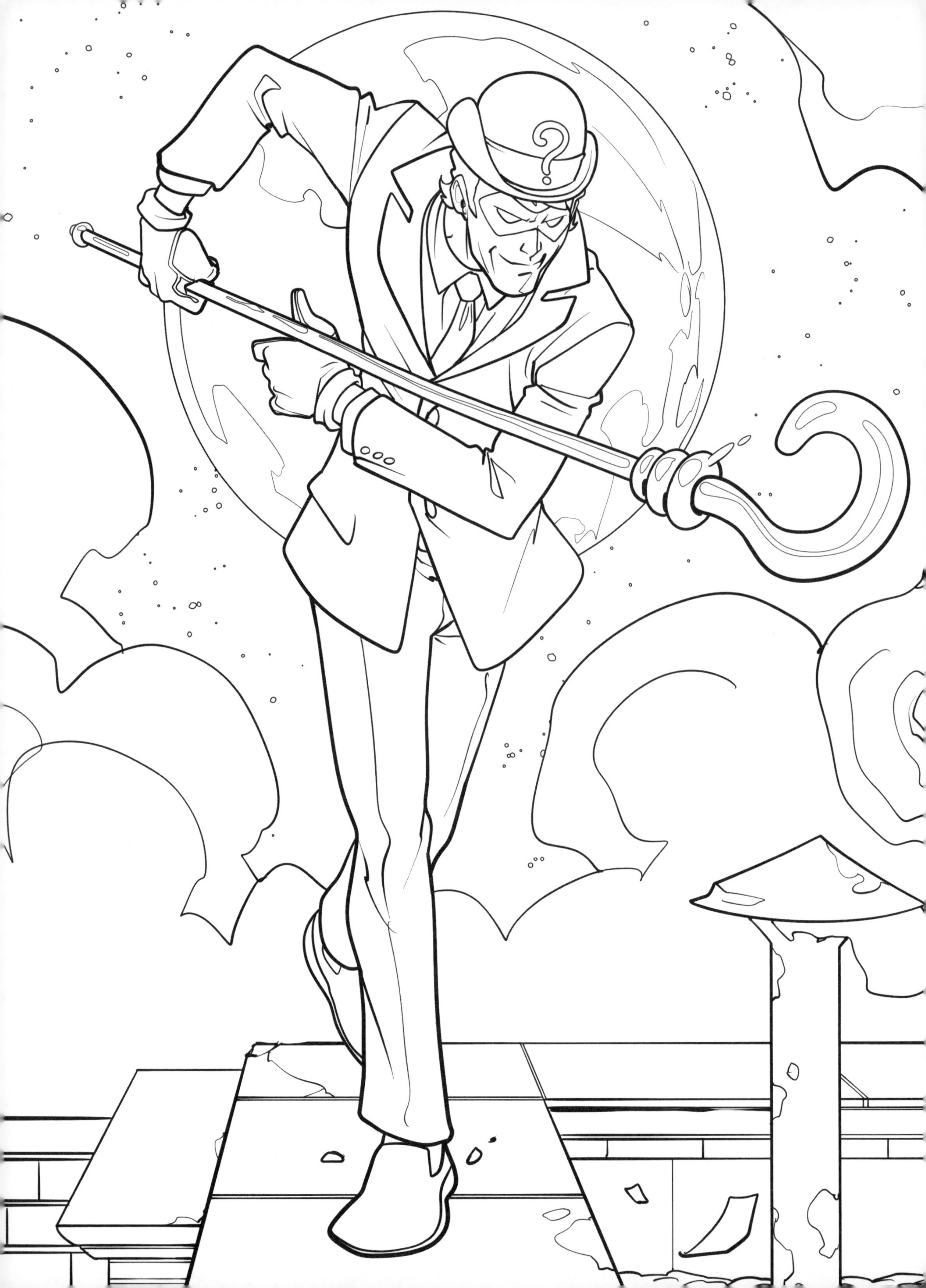

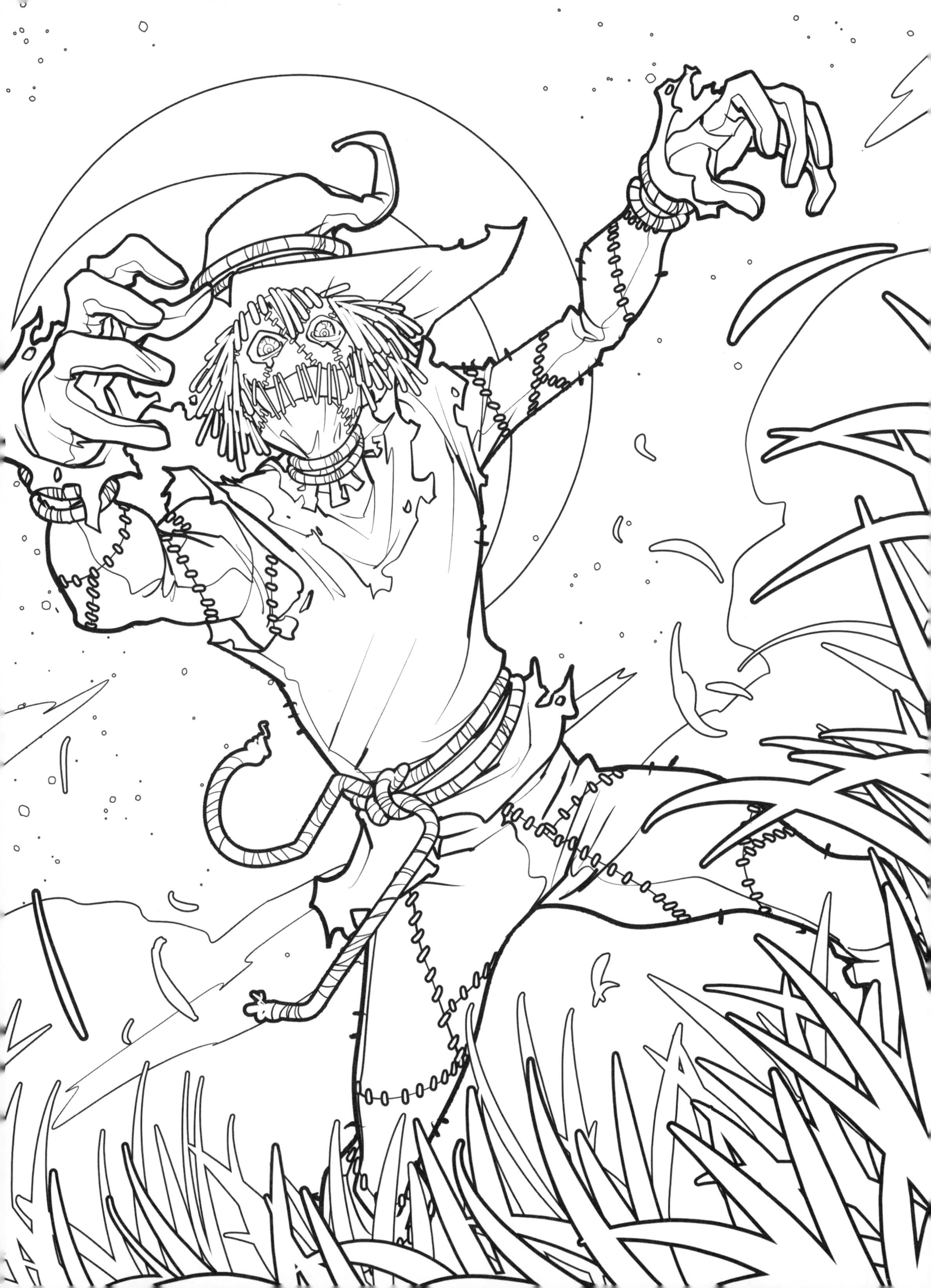

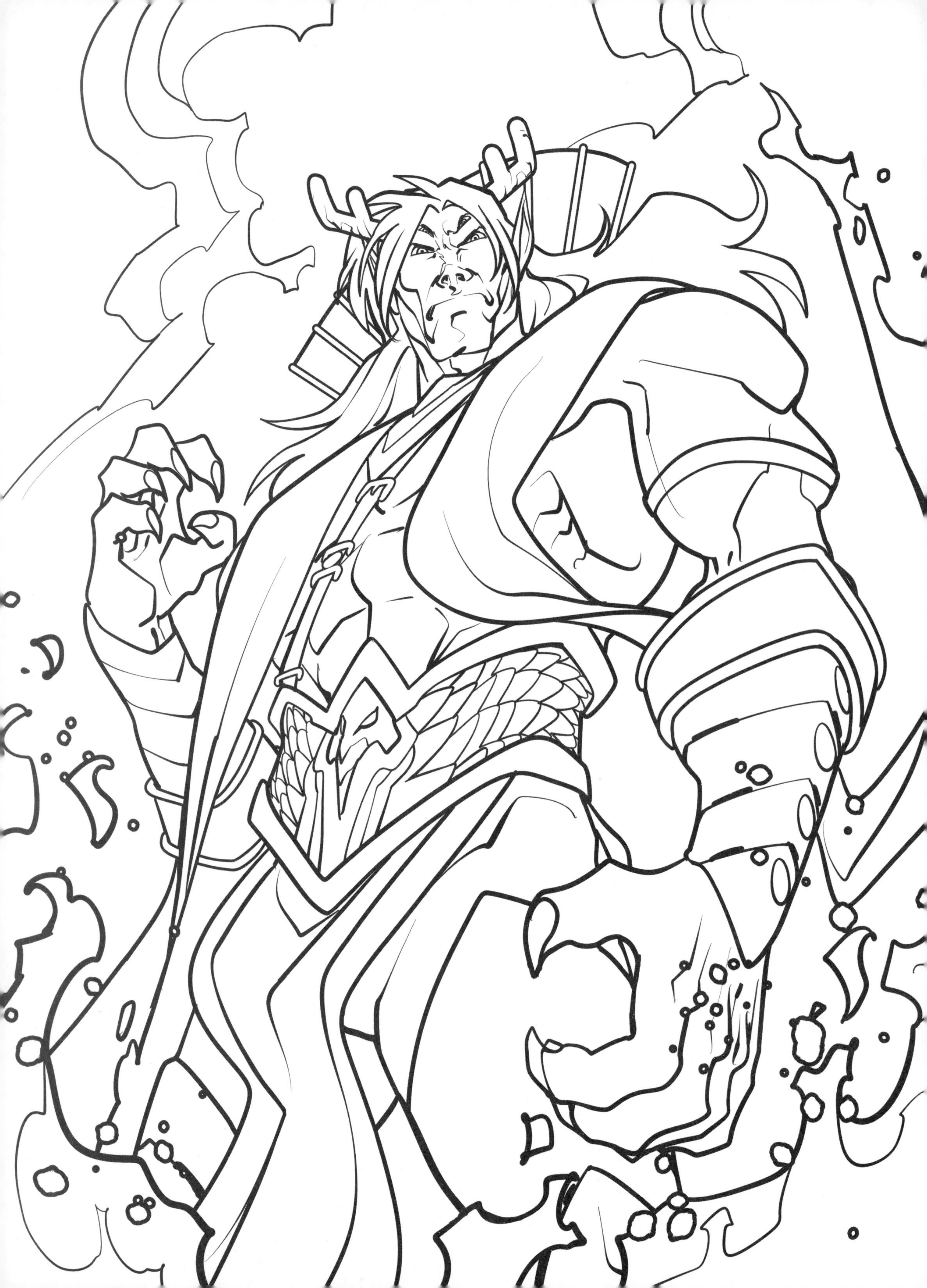

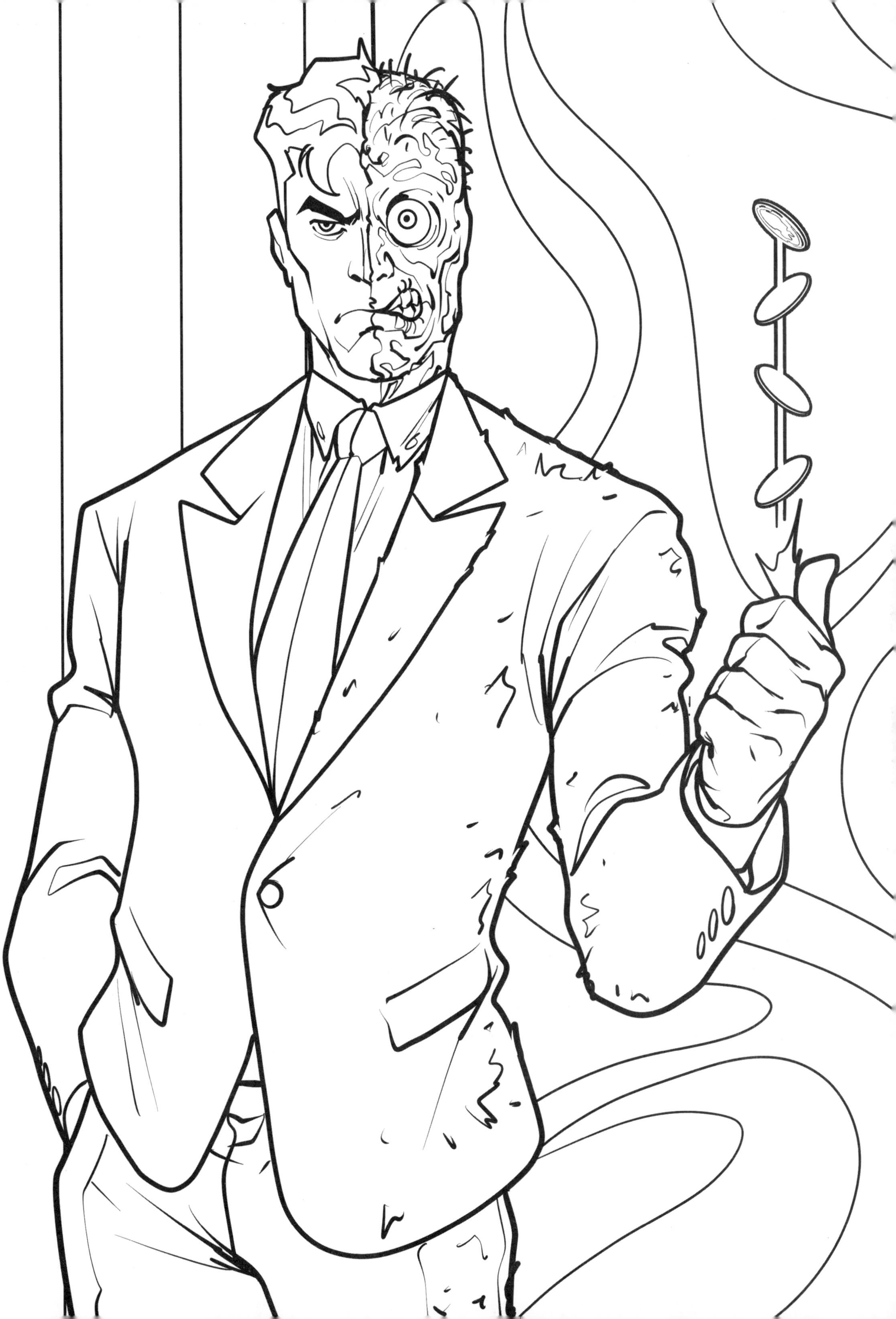

INSIGHT
EDITIONS
PO Box 3088
San Rafael, CA 94912
www.insighteditions.com

Find us on Facebook: www.facebook.com/InsightEditions
Follow us on Twitter: @insighteditions

Published by Insight Editions, San Rafael, California, in 2023.

ISBN: 979-8-88663-102-9

Publisher: Raoul Goff
VP, Co-Publisher: Vanessa Lopez
VP, Creative: Chrissy Kwasnik
VP, Manufacturing: Alix Nicholaeff
VP, Group Managing Editor: Vicki Jaeger
Publishing Director: Jamie Thompson
Design Manager: Megan Sinead Bingham
Senior Editor: Justin Eisinger
Editorial Assistant: Sami Alvarado
Managing Editor: Maria Spano
Senior Production Editor: Michael Hylton
Production Associate: Tiffani Patterson
Senior Production Manager, Subsidiary Rights: Lina s Palma-Temena

Illustrations by José Carlos Silva

ROOTS of PEACE REPLANTED PAPER
Insight Editions, in association with Roots of Peace, will plant two trees for each tree used in the manufacturing of this book. Roots of Peace is an internationally renowned humanitarian organization dedicated to eradicating land mines worldwide and converting war-torn lands into productive farms and wildlife habitats. Roots of Peace will plant two million fruit and nut trees in Afghanistan and provide farmers there with the skills and support necessary for sustainable land use.

Manufactured in China by Insight Editions

10 9 8 7 6 5 4 3 2